ALSO BY JORGE GARCÍA-ROBLES PUBLISHED
BY THE UNIVERSITY OF MINNESOTA PRESS

The Stray Bullet: William S. Burroughs in Mexico

AT THE END OF THE ROAD

AT THE END OF THE ROAD

JACK
KEROUAC

IN MEXICO

JORGE GARCÍA-ROBLES

TRANSLATED BY
DANIEL C. SCHECHTER

UNIVERSITY OF MINNESOTA PRESS

MINNEAPOLIS • LONDON

Originally published in Spanish as *El disfraz de la inocencia: La historia de Jack Kerouac en México* (Mexico City: Ediciones del Milenio, 2000) and later republished in *Burroughs y Kerouac: Dos forasteros perdidos en México* (Mexico City: Random House Mondadori, 2007). Copyright 2006 Jorge García-Robles and copyright 2007 Random House Mondadori, S.A. de C.V.

Selections of poetry by Jack Kerouac are reprinted by permission of SLL/Sterling Lord Literistic, Inc. Copyright by John Sampas, Literary Representative.

English translation copyright 2014 by the Regents of the University of Minnesota

Published by the University of Minnesota Press
111 Third Avenue South, Suite 290
Minneapolis, MN 55401–2520
http://www.upress.umn.edu

Library of Congress Cataloging-in-Publication Data
García-Robles, Jorge.
At the end of the road : Jack Kerouac in Mexico /
Jorge García-Robles ; translated by Daniel C. Schechter.
Includes bibliographical references.
ISBN 978-0-8166-8064-1 (hc)— ISBN 978-0-8166-8065-8 (pb)
1. Kerouac, Jack, 1922–1969—Travel—Mexico. 2. Authors, American—
20th century— Biography. 3. Americans—Mexico—Biography.
4. Beat generation—Biography. I. Schechter, Daniel C., translator. II. Title.
PS3521.E735Z632913 2014   813'.54—dc23
[B]
2014019927

Printed in the United States of America on acid-free paper

The University of Minnesota is an equal-opportunity educator and employer.

20 19 18 17 16 15 14   10 9 8 7 6 5 4 3 2 1

Man is a stream whose source is hidden.

— RALPH WALDO EMERSON

And nowhere that we went was far: the earth and the sky were close and near. And the old hunger returned—the terrible and obscure hunger that haunts and hurts Americans, and that makes us exiles at home and strangers wherever we go.

— THOMAS WOLFE

"I will have no man in my boat," said Starbuck, "who is not afraid of a whale."

— HERMAN MELVILLE

CONTENTS

PREFACE TO THE U.S. EDITION

After his own, Mexico was perhaps the single most important country in Jack Kerouac's life. Between 1950 and 1961, he trod *tierra mexicana* six or seven times. While here, he wrote an entire novel, *Dr. Sax*, half of *Tristessa*, parts of *Maggie Cassidy* and *Desolation Angels*, and three volumes of poetry: *Mexico City Blues*, *Orizaba 210 Blues*, and "Cerrada Medellín Blues." Mexico figured abundantly and significantly in his correspondence, and it was during his creative peak, the 1950s, that he repeatedly sojourned there.

Comparing Kerouac's Mexico visits to those of other American and European writers who made similar journeys to the country in the twentieth century, it becomes clear that his mode of travel was unique. Aleister Crowley, though he never expected much of Mexico, enjoyed his stay there and always spoke positively of his Mexican experiences; Graham Greene hated Mexico before and after he encountered it; D. H. Lawrence, Malcolm Lowry, and William S. Burroughs were initially enthused but ultimately disappointed by it; Antonin Artaud detested mestizo Mexico while praising its indigenous–Tarahumara side (though he went insane soon after his trip); and to André Breton, who saw Mexico from the safe distance of the pampered tourist, it was neither good nor bad . . .

Kerouac had already formed a more or less preconceived notion

ix

of Mexico before he ever went there. Fellahin Mexico was a poor land with a greater interest in the spiritual world than the material one, that is, a realm akin to his own religious (at that time, Buddhistic) quest. Traveling to Mexico meant inhabiting a space unlike that of his native land, the United States, toward which he held contradictory feelings. On the one hand, he felt part of it, defended certain traditional values, and in his novels created heroes who remain American archetypes; on the other, he was disgusted by his country's conventionality and did all he could to get away from it. In light of those conflicting feelings, Mexico represented a completely different culture, one still unpolluted by the loss of spiritual identity that, as Jack saw it, plagued the United States.

Throughout his life, Kerouac clung to this idyllic image of Mexico, as depicted first and foremost in his novels and travel chronicles, less so in his correspondence. Yet this spiritual, almost redemptive Mexico (as portrayed in the final pages of *On the Road*) ran up against the writer's actual experiences, particularly in Mexico City, where he was generally extorted, assaulted, and harassed. Still, Kerouac strove to convert—quite literally—its sordidness into profundity, its repulsiveness into holiness. He never abandoned this beatific vision of Mexico because his literary blueprint demanded it. For Kerouac, Mexico was more of a literary invention than a real-life experience. He held fast to this idealized notion of Mexico not because he felt it but because within the literary universe he endeavored to create, this fellahin nation could be nothing else; describing it precisely as he experienced it, displaying both its good and bad sides, with all its contradictions, virtues, and defects, was not an option; making it into a literary scenario was.

The same might be said of Kerouac's entire body of work: that he not only invented and embellished Mexico with his literary designs but that all the places, situations, and people he re-created in his novels and stories were inventions, too—for which he must be forgiven, because Jack Kerouac, rather than a sociologist or journalist, was a writer and because, thankfully, rather than write to live he lived to write.

That said, Kerouac's actual and literary experiences in Mexico remain fascinating. In this book, which I wrote while steeped in all things Kerouacian, I set out to re-create from my research of all available documentation on the subject both the actual and literary experiences of Kerouac in "the hot country" of "the desert rats and the tequila." Still, I won't rule out the possibility that, just as the author of *Mexico City Blues* wove a Mexico from his fantasies, I conjured a Kerouac from my own. Maybe there is no other way; literature (and life) is the stuff of imagination and fantasy, not absolute truth.

For those who can tune in to the frequency and tap the energy of this universal American author—prophet of his generation without ever meaning to be, fabricator of a vast literary oeuvre that remains vital and current more than half a century later—experiencing his Mexican adventures should prove a passionate journey well worth taking.

J. G.-R., MEXICO CITY, 2014

AT THE END OF THE ROAD

1

My life is a vast and insane legend reaching everywhere

without beginning or ending, like the Void . . .

—JACK KEROUAC, *Desolation Angels*

Lowell, Massachusetts, March 12, 1922. Under the sign of Pisces (sign of the idealistic, conflicted, selfish, and hypersensitive), with Leo rising, Jean-Louis Kerouac was born, the third son of Leo Alcide Kerouac and Gabrielle Levesque, both Quebeckers recently emigrated to New England. Papa Leo worked at a printing press, Memère Gabrielle in a shoe factory. The Québécois French spoken by the lower-middle-class family had a heavy Catholic accent. The Kerouacs never missed a Sunday mass. Jack had two siblings: Gerard, five years older than he, and Carolyn, three years older. Gerard died at age nine from a lung disease, and his death marked Jack for the rest of his days. Gerard was to become a highly valued item in the family museum. He was held up as a sort of Holy Child of Atocha, canonized, beatified, and stigmatized as the incarnation of good. Jack obsessively emulated his anointed brother. Memère was most responsible for the canonization of the dead child. Once she reproached Ti Jean (Jack), saying, "It should've been you that died, not Gerard." The vulnerable Jack had few resources to defend himself against such an onslaught, and his unconscious mind was stamped and sealed with the guilt of not being his brother's equal.

He also inhaled the familiar odor of Catholicism at school and with his friends. But the young Jack did not reject such apostolic, Roman paraphernalia. He accepted and embraced it with such fervor that in his room he sometimes had Claudelian visions—more paranoiac than revelatory—of the Messiah and the Virgin Mary. It was torture confessing his onanistic experiences to the priest, and early on he stumbled on an equation that he would never solve as he mixed up true faith with guilt, morality with the desire to transcend the world, pleasure with debt. Jack was never good at the mathematics of life. Rather than solve problems, he relished or pondered them, like a good writer.

Jack was an imaginative child. He read, wrote, made up games, and created his own world outside the strictures of morality. He was sociable and played with his friends. He listened to the radio adventures of Dick Tracy and Flash Gordon, went to the movies, and played football. In his teenage years, he excelled as a quarterback. Mary Carney was his first girlfriend, though he never made love to her. He invented Dr. Sax, about whom he'd write a novel sixteen years later in Mexico. He met Sebastian "Sammy" Sampas, a poet of Greek heritage and his posthumous brother-in-law (in 1966 Sampas's sister became Kerouac's third wife), who recommended he read Thomas Wolfe, a key literary influence. After graduating high school, he got a grant to play football and study at Columbia. His

2

parents swelled with hope and pride. Their imaginative and somewhat scatterbrained son might go on to become an American champ. Lacking such ambitions, or rather wide-eyed and open to whatever came his way, Jack Kerouac left Lowell for New York in 1939 and set out on the road.

BELLY OF THE BEAST

New York turned out to be the igneous substratum for the eruption of the previously dormant Jack Kerouac. The contrast between the Big Apple and his hometown opened his provincial eyes, broadened his narrow outlook, and aired the myrrh and incense from his room. This was nothing like life in Lowell. A new world was revealing itself to him. For one, he discovered the black universe. At the Apollo Theater, myocardium of Harlem, he heard jazz and it moved him. Its phrasing, beat, spasms, spontaneity, and flow awakened within him a sensibility he had never known existed. It astonished him, in contrast to white music, which now just seemed vapid. He began to reject all the frivolous expressions of middle-class America, so comfortable yet empty, so safe yet ruinous, where matter triumphed over the spirit, the utilitarian over the creative, the obtuse over the diverse. Jazz was the opposite of all that. It moved like a bird, soaring with complete freedom, flowed with a protean, richly symbolic sonority. Improvisation, the art of becoming, not repeating (the true father of jazz isn't Parmenides but Heraclitus) became an ethical and aesthetic axiom. Eventually Kerouac's life and work would overlap with the rituals of jazz. His Catholicism and Buddhism were more deeply inspired by jazz than Gospels or sutras. More than words, his articles of faith had sheet music. He also got acquainted with New York's lower depths, saved up his money, and lost his virginity to a red-headed prostitute. He read Whitman and when the Second World War broke out discovered Goethe's *Faust*, which moved him, and Dostoyevsky, which hit him like an exploding sun.

But New York was also an antirevelation. Worms crept out of the Big Apple. America in the 1940s was not the promised land dreamt of by Whitman or by the pioneers of the seventeenth century. At least not for the sensitive young Kerouac, for whom the American Dream turned sour in New York.

The American Dream, the supreme myth of Yankee culture, the totem before which North American civilization kneels, symbol of hope and purpose for millions of bedazzled souls who arrived on America's shores as if they were lining up for Noah's Ark and embarking on a journey that would sooner or later grant their wishes for wealth and freedom. Long live the New World! (Cue in the second movement of Dvorak's New World Symphony.) Long live the land of opportunity! shrieked the emigrants from the grungy decks of the *Mayflower* as they left the Old World behind and spat in its face, even if they inherited its whole slew of customs and obsessions. (The African emigrants to America were not exactly in pursuit of a dream.) Soul adventurers, self-sacrificing Lutherans, straitlaced Calvinists, unpolluted Puritans, romantic losers, prophets of democracy and progress, incorrigible rascals, compulsive gold diggers, optimistic freethinkers, ultra entrepreneurs, poets of dubious habits—in short, risk takers . . . all traveling with a suitcase full of dreams, all heading for the country that, they thought, would fulfill their yearnings. In coming together they erected a giant chimera (all too real) whose result was the USA. The American Dream became an irresistible seduction for millions, all wanting to taste the promise of a definitive solution to history. In God We Trust . . . but God is us, men of flesh and blood with the will to build our utterly earthly destiny. God didn't die, but his home is a level below our temporary dreams. The act of succumbing to this temptation led to the installation on American soil of the most frightfully starry-eyed country that had ever existed and the emergence of a super-tribe that deliriously strove to enact the Faustian liturgy of modern times: to make man, in Ptolemaic fashion, the navel of the universe. There in New York, young Jack intuited that the American Dream was an absurd race against time, in which the greatest terror was death, which is to say, the death of time, and in which eternity was replaced by a nice cold Coca-Cola.

By the nineteenth century, the USA's golden age, Herman Melville was perfectly aware of all that. Captain Ahab is the American Dream crashing into a superior reality, which it desired but was unable to dominate. Beneath the *Pequod*, that Faustian craft with "USA" on its side, an enormous white cetacean prowls, as if to remind its crew of the risks of indiscriminate dreaming: while Whitman waxed poetic over the American Dream ("The United States themselves are essentially the greatest poem," he claimed, beard to the wind), it was Melville who thoroughly understood the essence of the country that most feared death and thus fled most readily from a reality that could not be perceived via iris and retina.

And Kerouac's dreams were more akin to those of the white whale than Captain Ahab; more like those of a mendicant monk who anxiously looks into himself than of a typical middle-class gringo who dreams only of climbing the social ladder and making his first million, thus avoiding the social or psychological ruin of being stigmatized as a loser. Loserdom is the greatest sin an American can commit, the worst of deficiencies, the most unpardonable of errors. For the average American, to lose is to condemn oneself to a hell where those who cannot realize their grandiose dreams are sent, to be kicked off the playing field while the flock harshly boos these failures and disqualifies their existence. A veritable racetrack of social competition.

At age nineteen, Jack Kerouac walked down Broadway, crossed Forty-Seventh Street, looked up, glimpsed the neon of Times Square, observed the Camels ad, looked at a man clutching a briefcase and adjusting his glasses, at a woman entranced by a fashion store window, at a young man in a gray flannel suit heading determinedly to Wall Street as hundreds of cars advanced like fugitives. He stopped suddenly, moved his head, twisted his mouth, swallowed, felt a pang in his heart, a torrent of adrenaline in his belly. For the first time, he surmised that he was unlike others. For the first time, he was informed of his incompatibility with the narrow world of men. On that day, Jack entered the brotherhood of wayward geniuses, people as talented as they were unable to live in peace, tormented visionaries who paid dearly for their inspiration. Poe, E.T.A. Hoffman, Leopardi, van Gogh, London, Fitzgerald, La Rochelle, Artaud, Hart Crane, Modigliani, Hölderlin, Lowry, Dylan Thomas, Mayakovsky, Schumann . . . Jack Kerouac. (Not Burroughs or Ginsberg, who belonged to another equally marginal, though not tragic, brotherhood.) Crippled visionaries of the soul whose imagination ran like fallow deer but needed crutches to advance in real life. To be damned but not blind, as William Carlos Williams put it, that was both their sentence and their salvation. To be with men but not to be with them. Never in harmony. Not to live within God but to imagine him or desire him hysterically, such was the unconfessed, existential catechism of Jack Kerouac, one of the last damned visionaries, and the first to herald a new brand of twenty-first-century mysticism.

American civilization was despicable indeed, but Jack Kerouac, an American after all, still enjoyed sinking his teeth into it—even if he didn't have much faith in it. Young Jack's character was a mix of anguish and wanton exploit, introspection and feverish activity, existential doubt and vital entropy. A tragic finger pointed at Jack, but that didn't render him inactive. On the contrary, he directed his youthful energies toward outlandish experience, even where conventional behavior prevailed.

He started drinking. At Columbia he played football and took courses in Shakespeare. He excelled at the game but broke his leg in a tackle. While he was recovering at the hospital he got into *Look Homeward, Angel* by Thomas Wolfe. He was elected vice president of his class, appeared in school publications, passed chemistry, and got As in French. He spent the summer with his friends in Lowell—some hell-raisers, others intellectual poets. He'd chase women, drink and carry on with some of them, discover *Ulysses* and *The Decline of the West*, write stories, and take lengthy walks till dawn with others. Back in New York and fed up with Columbia, he decided to drop out of academia and football. University studies didn't fulfill him. Real life was outside the classroom. Sports didn't quench his lust for life. His parents' world fell apart. The son who had shown such promise wasn't panning out. He was becoming conflictive, volatile, full of incomprehensible urges. Seeing Jack's melancholic stare they asked, What does he want? By way of reply he shrugged his shoulders, raised his eyebrows, turned around, and, with a black angel hovering over him and his hands stuck in the pockets of his wrinkled chinos, left that world behind with nothing more than some dreams quite unlike those of his compatriots and a blank notebook stuffed into his rear pocket.

A SUPRALITERARY TRINITY

In 1942, Jack did odd jobs and set out for Greenland with the merchant marine, signing on for a three-month stint as a ship's mate. Thus began his transient course of taking to the road as an end in itself. From that time forward, the goal of any journey would be the journey itself, to flow rather than stagnate, change rather than define. Heraclitus was the first Beat philosopher, Apollonius of Tyana the first Beat mystic of the early Christian era, Casanova a sybaritic Beat of the eighteenth century, Rimbaud a damned Beat of the nineteenth. The road was the thing—the journey, not the destination. The only point in arriving was to set off again.

When Kerouac returned from Greenland, he spent a few days with his parents in Lowell. The coach of his football team asked him to come back to Columbia. He accepted, and while he studied and trained he plumbed Harlem's lower depths and listened to jazz, smoked marijuana, and took Benzedrine. Visiting him in New York, Sammy Sampas, his best friend from Lowell, was shocked and reproached him. Jack responded in Rimbaudian style that a writer had to taste excess to obtain a deep knowledge of existence. At age twenty, he began his romance with consciousness-altering substances.

A short time later he dropped out of Columbia. He could no longer take either the classroom or the playing field. No academics, no profession. Fate had something else in mind for him. He decided to be a writer. A sanguine writer, out to equate the written word with life's diastoles.

At the beginning of 1943, in the middle of a world war, he enlisted in the marines. He was sent to Newport, Rhode Island, but he hated military hierarchy from the outset and refused to become a combat soldier and conveniently kill the enemy. He beat up an officer who had struck him, disobeyed orders, foiled discipline in numerous ways. His superiors ran him through psychological tests and confined him to a hospital with other crazy insubordinates. Jack gave them a grandiloquent harangue on the impossibility of his submitting to discipline, and induced the doctors to diagnose him as schizophrenic. Finally, he was granted leave. A farewell to arms. Neither war nor the army was in the cards.

Far from fading, his wanderlust overcame him and weeks later he set sail for Liverpool, once again on a transatlantic merchant ship. The ship held a cargo of five hundred bombs. When the proximity of German subs was loudly broadcast, the unperturbed Jack lay in his bunk. And with no women around, he had sex with the other seamen. In his spare moments, he revised an attempted novel titled *The Sea Is My Brother*. Arriving in England, he visited the notorious brothels of London and Liverpool (where he might have seen a three-year-old child named John playing in the park with his aunt Mimi), got drunk, and attended a Tchaikovsky concert at the Royal Albert Hall, air raids included.

Back in New York, like Ulysses landing, he rushed headlong for the subway to find the house of Frankie Edith Parker, with whom he'd had something more than a fling months earlier and whom he'd promised to move in with as soon as he returned. He arrived at 421 West 118th Street, climbed six flights of stairs, and knocked. Edie opened the door, greeted him enthusiastically, made him dinner (asparagus with mayonnaise), made the bed. The two spent a torrid night together, the start of a white-hot love affair. Kerouac stuck around and lived in the flat. He liked Edie's vivaciousness—he liked anyone's vivaciousness. They went to the movies, ate at German restaurants. Edie usually paid. Her family—from Grosse Pointe, Michigan, was wealthy. In the Village he chatted with James T. Farrell and Ernest Hemingway. He went to Harlem to hear jazz, saw Charlie Parker and Dizzy Gillespie perform. Nights Jack banged on his typewriter. Sometimes Jack and Edie went to Ozone Park, where Jack's parents had moved. Memère was not pleased that her boy was living with a little girl, sweet as she was but too modern.

Edie lived with a girlfriend, Joan Vollmer, born in Albany. Nineteen years old. Brilliant, sarcastic, with a lovely porcelain face, cerulean eyes, a perverse, faraway gaze. Hard living, into sex, a voracious reader. And right around the time when Truman Capote was dining with Gloria Vanderbilt and Oona O'Neill at El Morocco, and J. D. Salinger was doing military counterintelligence for the army, Edie's friend Lucien Carr, a Columbia student with the look of a Macedonian youth, brought another man of seventeen to the apartment. He wore thick, black glasses, had a stunned expression and bulging lips. Born in New Jersey of a Russian-Jewish mother, he was an intelligent youth and a closet homosexual. They said he was a union leader who also studied at Columbia. His name was Allen Ginsberg. A little while later, also through Lucien Carr, Jack met a bizarre specimen, aged thirty, with a reptilian face, an impassive look and aristocratic ways. A Harvard grad. He was missing his left pinky. Cynically bored with life, a budding consumer of opiates, he expressed his dissatisfaction through black humor. William S. Burroughs. For those who like to watch fireworks shooting skyward, the meet-up of Kerouac, Ginsberg, and Burroughs was among the most opportune in twentieth-century (supra)literary culture. (For those who don't—academics, pseudo-aesthetes, theoreticians, and mega-intellectuals—it was no more than a revved-up encounter between three wacky gringos.) Kerouac, Ginsberg, and Burroughs formed a supraliterary trinity, who, together with other shamans, would incubate a supracultural movement that was unprecedented in history. Burroughs would be the father, Kerouac the son, and Ginsberg the Holy Ghost . . . God and his pack of rebels, bless 'em.

Spontaneously formed, without prior notice, without a game plan, without a notarized birth certificate, without press conferences or official notification, the West 118th Street (later 115th Street) clan became the uterus for an embryo that would gestate a few years later. Subsequent additions to the fold included drug addict and writer Herbert Huncke, anthropology/archaeology student Hal Chase, the impish Baudelairean Lucien Carr, and various hangers-on. The new androgynous-mystical-Aquarian code that traveled so far in the 1960s had its larval form in this apartment, where a new filter was being developed for the conception and experience of life in an utterly unaccustomed fashion. It amounted to an antisolemn alternative for living, a patent rejection of the era's civilized habits, and it entailed sexual freedom, recreational and self-cognitive use of consciousness-altering substances, adherence to nature, love for adventure and travel, cultivation of a fringe wisdom, renouncement of conventional relationships, creation of an art free of artifice, contact with above-life planes . . . a whole caravan of antiartificial attitudes available to anyone unable to reside in the minuscule corral where the human super-tribe grazed, curiously proud of the hyper-advanced technology it had developed without noticing that its generic condition had remained unchanged from twenty thousand years earlier.

Still, there were excesses. Burroughs and the others compulsively consumed hard drugs, which they scored in New York's lower depths. And Lucien Carr stabbed David Kamerer to death after the redhead, hopelessly infatuated with Carr, sexually harassed him. Tired of the harassment, Lucien, in a fit of rage, plunged a dagger into the obsessed youth, then dragged his body to the Hudson and went running off in search of Burroughs and Kerouac. The supportive, naive Kerouac helped him conceal the evidence—the knife and Kamerer's glasses. Later, they both went to the movies to calm down and take their minds off the incident. But Carr couldn't stand the pressure and, two days later, turned himself in. The police locked up his two friends for covering up the crime. After some investigation, the authorities determined that the accomplices could be released on paying a one-hundred-dollar fine. Burroughs's family paid, but not Kerouac's. Jack's father snorted upon learning that his son was wrapped up in such mischief and refused to put up the hundred bucks. Edie's family was willing to hand over the money on the condition that Jack marry her. As Jack had no other option, he agreed. Still a prisoner, he was allowed out to go to city hall and get married for the first time. He spent his honeymoon behind bars. Once released, he and his brand-new, if not exactly virginal, bride went to the home of his in-laws in Grosse Pointe, Michigan, where he pledged to find work so he could pay back the hundred-dollar loan.

The house of his new family was lavishly furnished, and the environment and customs contrasted with the simpler, run-of-the-mill ways of the recently arrived son-in-law. Jack felt ill at ease. He duly complied with certain formalities: get-togethers, meals, strolls. He slept with one of his wife's friskier friends, went to bars after his shift at Chrysler, read in public libraries, and after two months of married life, fed up and disgusted, told Edie he was going back to New York, *by himself*. Good-bye, Ruby Tuesday. The complacency of marriage and family life rubbed him the wrong way. Jack Kerouac had no tolerance for a comfortable, routine, tidy, dull way of life. The wayward writer preferred darkness to artificial light. The young Kerouac fled from stagnant living, preferring the challenge of navigating labyrinths to the security of the fireside, social standing, and proper manners. His spirit opted always to ply uncharted waters to maintain the tension that came with new terrain. The point was to weave experiences, unravel and reweave them, take to the road, and never settle down. When Jack stopped moving, he would begin dying.

Abandoning an acceptable marriage—he never returned to Edie —a good family, and a reputable status was simply Jack Kerouac's affirmation of his transient course and his need to poetize his life as intensely as he experienced it.

Back in New York, Jack lived temporarily with Burroughs and Joan Vollmer, who had begun a strange quasi-amorous connection there on 115th Street. His relationship with Ginsberg and Hal Chase intensified. They read, conversed. Burroughs and Jack wrote a story titled "And the Hippos Were Boiled in Their Tanks," inspired by the stabbing of Kamerer. He lost himself in the human zoo of New York, tore himself open under the spiritual guidance of the trinity's senior member ("Bill, whom I love dementedly," Jack wrote to Allen, "has the grandest mirror in which I can stare at myself"). They had occasional sex with each other, discovered Buddhism and its emptinesses, consumed Benzedrine, opiates, marijuana, and alcohol to such an extent that Jack developed phlebitis and had to spend time in a hospital, where he wrote and got into Stendhal's *The Red and the Black* and Goethe's *Poetry and Truth*. Ginsberg fell in love with Jack, who, though the feeling wasn't mutual, slept with him in the Columbia dorm. One night they were caught in bed together and Allen was kicked out of New York's most highly renowned university (ever since the Carr–Kamerer incident, Jack was considered persona non grata among the Columbia student community).

In 1946, Jack moved back in with Memère in Queens and began to write what would be his first novel, *The Town and the City*, a chronicle of his youth. It was his debut, and his literary muscle had yet to appear. Daily, before writing, Jack knelt and prayed, and while his mother labored in a factory, Jack took care of his embittered father, who had stomach cancer, felt terribly frustrated, and held a recalcitrant, caustic view of blacks, Jews, drug addicts, and bums, among whom he obviously included Ginsberg, Burroughs and other bad apples who threatened to pervert his only, easily swayed son. A bit later, he died; the event added new guilt entries to the log of Jack's subconscious.

Later that year, a friend of Hal Chase arrived from Denver, supposedly to study at Columbia: Neal Cassady, born on the same day as James Dean. Chase introduced him to the topsy-turvy world of the 115th Street flat. Cassady arrived in New York with precious few dollars and a sixteen-year-old bombshell of a wife, Luanne, a willowy brat with a sculpted figure, straight hair, and a feeble mind. The twenty-year-old Neal had been in and out of reformatories and prisons since childhood for auto theft and other crimes. But besides trampling and spitting on societal norms he also read Nietzsche, Dostoyevsky, Dickens, Kant, and Thomas Wolfe, had hitchhiked around a large part of the country, had high testosterone levels that impelled him to unload his sexual energies as copiously and indiscriminately as he wished, and possessed certain aspirations to be a writer.

Little by little, Jack was finding both an ally and an archetype in Neal Cassady. Neal was to become Jack's ideal cohort, someone who shared his attitudes about life. Both men felt that the world was a pressure cooker holding in steam that needed to be released. Social norms were a hindrance to living life, conventions hardened the vital arteries. Soon after sizing each other up, they embarked on various adventures, following the Heraclitean-jazzistic imperative that Jack held up as the ethical epicenter of his life and literary work: tune in to evolving.

A series of indispensable dishes figured on the menu for the jazz-tracked adventures of Kerouac, Cassady, and their eventual travel companions (Ginsberg chief among them): speed and improvisation (like a dizzying Charlie Parker solo), a car, sedatives (alcohol, grass), stimulants (amphetamines), women, casual sex, a high degree of unscrupulousness, and an invariably playful attitude.

Neal Cassady became the key literary hero in Kerouac's oeuvre. For Jack, Cassady represented the archetype of the American male; and one of the literary motivations for the author of *Visions of Cody* was to mythologize America—not as an abstract and hopeful notion (as Whitman did) but as something pristine and lost (before the dream begot monsters), which Neal incarnated. The celebrated complicity between these two figures in the late 1940s and early 1950s was a milestone in the history of literature and the American (supra)culture. They wanted to suck the last drop out of life, and their behavior had the nature of a religious quest, mainly for Jack.

Apart from their affinities, they also had their differences. Cassady was basically an unscrupulous hell-raiser. Kerouac was an artist who wrote about the things he experienced. Each sought out and admired in the other what he himself lacked: Kerouac Neal's vitality and fearlessness, Neal Jack's intelligence and literary genius. Here were a volatile Dionysus and an unbalanced Apollo, a pair of mismatched but eventually compatible personalities who despite their differences shared the drama of their fate, which would inevitably and prematurely hit a brick wall.

Jack found in Neal a suitable catalyst to spirit out his roving sign, and from 1947 onward, they set off on a series of epic car trips, from New York to San Francisco, Texas to Mexico City, Denver to South Carolina, New Orleans to Chicago. They did it for two reasons: to look into themselves, and to rack up experiences to write about. Fortunately for readers, it was mostly the latter.

In March 1950, Harcourt Brace published *The Town and the City*, Jack Kerouac's first novel. A weak effort in many ways, it was ignored by critics and sold poorly. Jack was disappointed, but his course as a writer was set. It was during this period of close involvement with Neal that he read the man's sweaty, hyperspontaneous letters, and the muses lifted a veil in the right part of his brain to reveal a spontaneous-dynamic-bop-jazzistic literary style, his aesthetic of experience. The idea was to concoct text at the same frequency and intensity as he experienced life. From then on, Jack's literature would be a sort of word extractor that made life a work of art, at least on paper.

Out on the road, 1950, in straight-ahead travel mode, hell-bound for America and Mexico, removed from all convention, scruffy and carefree, Jack discovered his literary vocation in a flash of spontaneous combustion. And together with his various cohorts (John Clellon Holmes, Al Hinkle, and Allen Ginsberg), he began to think about the profile of his generation, which in 1955 would be dubbed the Beat Generation: elusive, outrageous, anticonventional, beatific, mystical, seeking higher realities. The religious vein that Kerouac strove to incorporate into his life and work was being incubated during this era of uninterrupted movement. In those days, a simple phrase defined what would become his universal ideology: Love God and write it. That was it. And it was in this stage of his life that Mexico first appeared.

I'm not American, nor West European, somehow I feel

like an Indian, a North American exile in North America.

—Letter to John Clellon Holmes, October 12, 1952

In September 1949, Jack Kerouac got a letter from Mexico written by William S. Burroughs, who, fleeing from American justice following accusations of drug trafficking, went to Mexico City with Joan Vollmer. During the early months of his stay, Burroughs was fascinated by Mexico (later he'd be disappointed), and he was anxious for his cohorts to visit him. Shortly after his arrival, he wrote Jack:

> Mexico is very cheap. A single man could live good for $2 per day in Mexico City, liquor included. $1 per day anywhere else in Mexico. Fabulous whorehouses and restaurants. A large foreign colony. Cockfights, bullfights, every conceivable diversion. I strongly urge you to visit. I have a large apt. could accommodate you. Tell Neal to come too if he is heeled. I have to watch the $.
> (Harris, *The Letters of William S. Burroughs, 1945–1959*, 53, 56)

A few months after receiving Burroughs's tantalizing news, Neal and an old friend, Frank Jeffries, finally spread their wings and flew toward "the hot country" of "the desert rats and the tequila." Their decision was absolutely unplanned, sudden; it defied the logic of precaution, like the tingling of sudden desire.

Denver, Colorado. June 1950. Jack Kerouac and Neal Cassady got into a 1937 Ford, Neal's, with "the right-side door unhinged and tied on the frame. The right-side front seat was also broken, and you sat there leaning back with your face to the tattered roof." Neal started the car, accelerated, then floored the gas pedal, and the Ford bounded over the highway to the magical south. Sprawled out in the back of the car, snoring assonantly and exhaling an alcoholic mist, was Frank Jeffries, an old pal of Neal's, who'd chipped in a hundred bucks for travel expenses. The three were hung over—the night before, they'd gotten completely smashed—but rather than giving in to fatigue, they were fired up by their state of physical exhaustion, prodded by it to make their first trip south of the 27th parallel.

In a state of euphoria, driving like an "Ahab at the wheel," Neal put pedal to the metal and the vehicle groaned forward. They went down through Colorado, New Mexico, Texas, and after covering a thousand miles with as little rest as possible made it to Laredo, Texas, "the bottom and dregs of America where all the heavy villains sink." About to clear customs, where "you could feel the enormous presence of whole great Mexico and almost smell the billion tortillas frying and smoking in the night," the cautious Jack asked Neal to take the grass they had wrapped in a piece of paper and toss it out the window. Neal threw it away—unnecessarily. "The Mexicans looked at our baggage in a desultory way," Jack relates. "They weren't like officials at all. They were lazy and tender."

21

In 1925, Russian poet Vladimir Mayakovsky, a tragic figure and a firm believer in history, traveled to Mexico.

When he arrived in Veracruz and saw the little, sandal-shod Mexicans for the first time, he asked:

"And where are the Indians?"

"These are the Indians," they told me.

Until I was twelve years old, I dreamed of the Indians according to Fenimore Cooper and Mayne Reed. And there before my very eyes, those peacocks were turning into chickens. My first disillusionment was a harsh lesson. (Mayakovsky, *Mi descubrimiento de América*, 21)

But unlike the Bolshevik bard, Kerouac and Cassady were not disappointed. Coming into Nuevo Laredo, Tamaulipas, at three in the morning, they were witnessing Mexico for the first time in their lives, and although they'd only seen one of the most hideous, sweltering, and desolate cities in northern Mexico, they felt as if they'd arrived in holy Lhasa.

As dawn broke, they saw Mexicans with sombreros sitting on their patios looking like oriental dope addicts. They exchanged their dollars for pesos, amazed by the quantity of Mexican notes they received. They went into a restaurant, ordered beer and cigarettes at laughably low prices, watched the Mexican outcasts devouring shapeless tortillas with beans, and, far from disappointing them, Mexico's charms were a revelation.

Behind us lay the whole of America and everything Dean [Neal]
and I had previously known: about life, and life on the road. We
had finally found the magic land at the end of the road and we
never dreamed the extent of the magic. (*On the Road*, 276)

In his mind, Jack was beginning to concoct the mythic face of
Mexico, whose immediate, apparent freshness contrasted with the
hypercivilized, pragmatic civilization of America. After deciding to
head straight for Mexico City—they had almost thirteen hundred
miles to go—they crossed the Salado River and stopped in Sabinas
Hidalgo, about a hundred miles short of Monterrey. They drove
slowly up the main drag, looking at houses and shops, and soon saw
a couple of girls go by. Fascinated by their ease and openness, Neal
exclaimed:

We've finally got to heaven. It couldn't be cooler, it couldn't be
grander, it couldn't be *anything*. . . . There's no *suspicion* here,
nothing like that. Everybody's cool, everybody looks at you with
such straight brown eyes and they don't say anything, just look,
and in that look all of the human qualities are soft and subdued and
still there. Dig all the foolish stories you read about Mexico and
the sleeping gringo and all that crap—and crap about greasers and
so on—and all it is, people here are straight and kind and don't put
down any bull. (*On the Road*, 277–78)

Ecstatic over this tableau of humanity, so different from their
own land, the three travelers got back in the Ford and, determined
to reach the heart of their recently discovered terra nova, ancient

Tenochtitlán, they got on the Pan-American Highway and headed south toward Monterrey. Upon the rocky outcrops of the cliffs along the highway, they saw a single word, written in white paint: *Alemán* —surname of the monarch/president then in office, Pedro Páramo, serving his six-year term, the behavioral epitome of the corrupt Mexican, the classic cacique whose greed is disguised by officialdom. Innocent Jack could not decipher this symbol, nor did he want to. Neither he nor Neal had come to Mexico to conduct sociological studies or political critiques. Unlike the young Paul Bowles in Monterrey in 1938, clad in a well-fitted red shirt with a portrait of Stalin in the middle, handing out flyers demanding the expulsion of Trotsky from Mexico, Neal and Jack were no seekers of justice or social messiahs. Nor were they anything like John Reed, that believer in cut-rate utopias who spanned the globe sniffing out revolutionaries and in Mexico found a coarse, illiterate social struggler named Pancho Villa, the only rascal who ever managed to invade the USA. The vital interests of Kerouac and Cassady revolved not around a political or ideological definition of the world. Jack had never really been interested in politics or social criticism, and he never passed judgment, as did Graham Greene, for whom "the Mexican Revolution was phony from the start." The political polarization of the Cold War, in which two empires clashed over the fate of planet Earth during the 1950s, did not concern him much. The innocent and spiritual Jack never viewed Mexico's authoritarianism, social injustice, exploitation, etc., through a critical, interrogating lens. For Jack Kerouac, Mexico was more a symbol than a country, a culture defined not at all by the ideological bent of its citizens or rulers but by the spirit of its people. What mattered to Kerouac was the souls of its denizens, their spiritual profile, not their social conditions. Eternity, not history. And so, if he'd glimpsed the name of the Mexican president whitewashed on a cliff side by the highway, it was just one more curious detail to mention.

As they came into Monterrey, the glitter of economic development overlay the rugged face of Mexico. The social space of the northern city was something of a hybrid, as industrial Mexico inevitably blended with underdeveloped Mexico—the innocent Mexico that seduced and charmed Jack and Neal. Without realizing it, in describing this contrast, Kerouac was describing Mexico's most salient feature: the imbalance between its wanting to be a modern nation, in the European or American sense of the term, and the psychological—not structural, social, or "historical"—impossibility of achieving it:

> Across this plateau the big manufacturing town of Monterrey sent smoke to the blue skies with their enormous Gulf clouds written across the bowl of day like fleece. Entering Monterrey was like entering Detroit, among great long walls of factories, except for the burros that sunned in the grass before them and the sight of thick city adobe neighborhoods with thousands of shifty hipsters hanging around doorways and whores looking out of windows and strange shops that might have sold anything and narrow sidewalks crowded with Hongkong-like humanity. (*On the Road*, 278–79)

Like the majority of European and American writers who traveled to Mexico in the first half of the twentieth century, Kerouac felt drawn not to the Mexico that drooled over the prospect of First

World membership but the Mexico that had been fired in pre-Hispanic kilns, in a non-Western mold. The savage Mexico, not the charming one, the wild Mexico rather than the dolled-up one. Not the incipiently industrial Mexico but the place of burros and straw mats. Not the one that wore ill-fitting clothes and tried to look like something it wasn't, that mimicked and (badly) copied political and economic schemes fashioned in mature Western societies—which, five years after the second world war, had only recently displayed their penchant for butchery—but the atavistic Mexico that was revealing itself to Kerouac as he drove the Ford down the highway outside Monterrey and went through Montemorelos, Linares, and Villa Hidalgo while Neal and Frank slept indulgently and obliviously in the back seat. In the following excerpt from *On the Road*—which the reader may excuse for its length—Jack Kerouac clearly expresses what Mexico meant to him from the mythic perspective on his first journey there:

> A great verdant jungle valley with long fields of green crops opened before me. Groups of men watched us pass from a narrow old-fashioned bridge. . . . The boys were sleeping, and I was alone in my eternity at the wheel, and the road ran straight as an arrow. Not like driving across Carolina, or Texas, or Arizona, or Illinois; but like driving across the world and into the places where we would finally learn ourselves among the Fellahin Indians of the world, the essential strain of the basic primitive, wailing humanity that stretches in a belt around the equatorial belly of the world from Malaya (the long fingernail of China) to India the great subconti-

nent to Arabia to Morocco to the selfsame deserts and jungles of Mexico and over the waves to Polynesia to mystic Siam of the Yellow Robe and on around, on around, so that you hear the same mournful wail by the rotted walls of Cadiz, Spain, that you hear 12,000 miles around in the depths of Benares the Capital of the World. These people were unmistakably Indians and were not at all like the Pedros and Panchos of silly civilized American lore— they had high cheekbones, and slanted eyes, and soft ways; they were not fools, they were not clowns; they were great, grave Indians and they were the source of mankind and the fathers of it. The waves are Chinese, but the earth is an Indian thing. As essential as rocks in the desert are they in the desert of "history." And they knew this when we passed, ostensibly self-important moneybag Americans on a lark in their land; they knew who was the father and who was the son of antique life on earth, and made no comment. For when destruction comes to the world of "history" and the Apocalypse of the Fellahin returns once more as so many times before, people will still stare with the same eyes from the caves of Mexico as well as from the caves of Bali, where it all began and where Adam was suckled and taught to know. These were my growing thoughts as I drove the car into the hot, sunbaked town of Gregoria. (*On the Road*, 280)

It would be difficult to find a more astute passage by a twentieth-century writer coming face-to-face with Mexico. Kerouac categorically distances himself from the typical crass American for whom the Mexicans—*fucking greasers*—were a bunch of filthy, ragged, sub-civilized tramps whose historical and racial stature was far beneath America's. Like Ginsberg and Burroughs, Kerouac detested the frivolousness and spiritual narrowness of the average gringo, a figure who, postwar, yearned for two shiny automobiles in the garage, as President Eisenhower had promised them, and desperately strove to triumph at the sport of amassing material wealth and social standing. In Kerouac's America, material concerns prevailed over spiritual ones, the lower over the higher, civilization over culture. Kerouac and his pals could not and would not enlist in this army of anthill builders, where freedom and creativity were replaced by apparent comfort and a frenzy to possess objects. As they saw it, the American Dream had become a nightmare—Moloch, for Ginsberg—which they must reject and subvert, each in his own way, in many different ways.

Thus, when they first encountered a much less civilized and therefore apparently more authentic and profound realm, Kerouac was somehow dazzled by it. The writer in the making, the anxious seeker, found in Mexico a sort of liberating Other, and not, as for many other Americans—even nonconformists—a mere touristic oddity of big straw sombreros and inedibly spicy dishes.

Kerouac used the term *fellahin*, which he'd taken from *The Decline of the West* by Oswald Spengler, to describe Mexicans and distinguish Mexico from other cultures, except that, while for Spengler the fellahin peoples populate those societies that outlive their own decadence, to Kerouac they were those who remained uninfluenced by the materialism of developed societies and thus preserved the origins of a profound, spiritual culture.

That said, what Mexico symbolized for Kerouac should not be seen as an organic, direct quest for indigenous Mexico, as it was for Antonin Artaud, who had studied the Mexican indigenous spirit and in 1934 went to Mexico "to make contact with Red Earth . . ." Nor was he like D. H. Lawrence, who in the twenties basked in the ancient traditions of Mexico, even as he noted the "curious, radical opposition of the Indians to the thing we call spirit"; or Jerzy Grotowski, who in 1979 went to the Sierra de Nayarit to live with the Huichols for several weeks as a basis for his Theater of Sources; or Carlos Castaneda, who went from being a curious academic to a devotee of the Toltec religious-initiatory tradition practiced by the Indians of Mexico's north; or even William S. Burroughs, who quite probably never had a conversation with a single indigenous Mexican though he read and had interest in the ancient Maya and Aztec cultures. It must be added that Kerouac's criterion for denominating certain Mexicans as Indians was more racial than cultural, as if to say that a black person from Harlem by just being black was a genuine Watusi. Jack, you may be forgiven your conceptual imprecision; we get the import of your quest.

Kerouac never seriously endeavored—as readers of the previous excerpt may surmise—to delve into the culture or traditions of Mexican Indians (or any others), either theoretically or physically. As much as he proclaimed them to belong to a sort of original race of humanity who were somehow wiser and more in harmony than other peoples, his interest in them was more a function of his stance against American civilization and its European roots than any real, vivid experience of sharing their cosmogony, customs, or visions of the world.

In reality, more than Mexico's indigenous people, what attracted him and what he always respected in all its sordidness and pettiness, was the hybrid Mexico, neither modern nor purely Indian. It was a blending that could seem as innocent, kind, and warmhearted as it was malicious, aggressive, and dangerous and which demonstrated a strange and ambiguous behavior toward the outside world that could be at once servile and violent, hospitable and vengeful, depending on the mood of the Mexican at hand, who was generally quite thin-skinned and fickle. Kerouac appreciated this mixed Mexico that was neither an ancient culture nor a modern civilization but the typical historical graft of countries that arrive late to modernity. This behavior, so apparent in 1950s Mexico, provided him with clear, abundantly empathetic points of reference that were more symbolic and literary than actual.

Another American writer, Jack London, though his life's pursuit had something in common with Kerouac's, held an altogether different opinion of Mexican mestizos. In Mexico to cover the invasion of Veracruz by the American army in 1914, he wrote: "they possess all the vices of their various commingled bloods and none of the virtues." Unlike Kerouac, London neither idealized nor forgave their shortcomings.

On the road to Mexico City, Kerouac, Cassady, and Jeffries stopped in Gregoria, Tamaulipas, where they met Victor, a barefoot youth who approached the Ford, hoping to sell them a windshield shade for sixty pesos.

"Nah, buy señorita?" Jack responded.

At the top of his voice, Victor told them he would get them girls, but later in the evening. Then Neal asked if he could sell them marijuana.

The youth said he could get them as much as they wanted and took them to the adobe hut of his mother, who gathered some recently cut marijuana leaves. Then they rolled up the weed in some scrap paper. It was the biggest joint that Jack had ever seen.

After smoking it with some of Victor's friends, there was an unspoken, mutually positive vibe among them, and they got in the car and headed for the roadhouse. They advanced fitfully owing to the abundance of potholes, ruts, and bumps in the road. Jack, feeling happy in his herb-induced state, summoned weird visions of Neal and Mexico that he related in *On the Road:*

> . . . Dean's [Neal's] face was suffused with an unnatural glow that was like gold as he told us to understand the springs of the car now for the first time and dig the ride. . . . he looked like God. I was so high I had to lean my head back on the seat; the bouncing of the car sent shivers of ecstasy through me. The mere thought of looking out the window at Mexico—which was now something else in my mind—was like recoiling from some gloriously riddled glittering treasure-box that you're afraid to look at because of your eyes, they bend inward, the riches and the treasures are too much

to take all at once. I gulped. I saw streams of gold pouring through the sky and right across the tattered roof of the poor old car. (*On the Road*, 284)

In another book, *Visions of Cody*, he describes the same scene, adding:

. . . he suddenly glowed up like a sun and became all rosy as a rosy balloon and beautiful as Franklin Delano Roosevelt . . . Cody [Neal] was so great, so good, that I couldn't believe—he was by far the greatest man I had ever known. . . . he's an angel. I'm his brother, that's all. (*Visions of Cody*, 298)

So here were Neal and Mexico, two sides of the same coin, Kerouac's cherished currency for transcending physical reality and entering other dimensions. With a little help from the grass, Jack leaped onto another plane, unleashed from fragmented reality, to rock upon an ever-yearned-for spiritual substratum of inner harmony, where Neal is God (as well as America in its purest state) and Mexico a magical land gushing golden symbols. What more could Jack, seeker and lover of alternative consciousness, ask for! The dual name Neal-Mexico echoed divinity.

Before reaching the eagerly anticipated whorehouse, where there'd be women, dancing, and booze—the basic ingredients for Dionysically altered consciousness—Victor stopped at his house to show them his six-month-old son. Seeing him, still overwhelmed with enchantment at everything that Mexico had lavished upon them, Neal exclaimed:

he is the prettiest child I have ever seen. . . . I want you par-ti-cu-lar-ly to see the eyes of this little Mexican boy who is the son of our wonderful friend Victor, and notice how he will come to man-hood with his own particular soul bespeaking itself through the windows which are his eyes, and such lovely eyes surely do proph-esy and indicate the loveliest of souls. (*On the Road*, 285)

Finally, just as dusk descended, they reached the bordello, where they binged tremendously on prostitutes and liquor. Out-side, two police with wrinkled trousers and bored expressions were sitting on the window sills. The bacchanal had Pérez Prado mam-bos as a sound track, all the rage in Mexico at the time. To Kerouac, the pulse of the mambo came straight from the heart of the world, a judgment that to the average mambo dancer of the period might have seemed overblown; Mexicans saw the mambo as just one more excuse to party rather than a quasi-religious sound:

"More Mambo Jambo," "Chattanooga de Mambo," "Mambo Nu-mero Ocho"—all these tremendous numbers resounded and flared in the golden, mysterious afternoon like the sounds you ex-pect to hear on the last day of the world and the Second Coming. The trumpets seemed so loud I thought they could hear them clear out in the desert, where the trumpets had originated anyway. The drums were mad. The mambo beat is the conga beat from Congo, the river of Africa and the world: it's really the world beat. (*On the Road*, 286)

After dancing as they'd never danced before, and drinking as usual, they had their way with several of the women working there and they exchanged partners, though Jack never had sex with the girl he most wanted: a dark-skinned sixteen-year-old who looked like a queen. Some random scruples kept either Cassady or Jeffries from approaching her. In the end, though they had thought their Mexican pesos would last indefinitely, the bill, as reported by Victor, was clearly too high—three hundred pesos, thirty-six dollars— but they didn't want to spoil things and did not dispute it. This was the first glimpse they'd had of Mexico's shadier side. But neither Jack nor the others said anything. The final scene of this episode could not have been more moving. Once they'd staggered into the car, thoroughly smashed, the hookers, roadhouse staff, and onlookers who'd observed the wild Americans through the cracks in the windows, gathered round the Ford. Praising, hugging, and kissing the passengers, in a pitch of excitement they bade them farewell. One of the whores even shed a few tears, the ever-inventive Jack noted on more than one occasion.

Before continuing their journey south, Victor took his slumming pals to a public bathhouse, where Jack and Frank—not Neal—took ice-cold showers and underwent a sort of rebirth. Saying good-bye to Victor and promising to return, Jack felt sorry to see "the sad park and the children" behind him. This was the Mexico that had seduced Jack: easy and physically exotic women, friendly cops, bizarre smells, unimaginable landscapes, strange music, and perhaps magical souls behind the unfamiliar faces and expressions, all crowned by a halo of profound sadness and mystery. Fellahin Mexico. To Jack, Mexico was a mixture of authenticity, magic, and melancholy, and he saw his own reflection though he may not have realized it.

Now hell-bound for Mexico City, they zoomed out of Gregoria, crossed the Tropic of Cancer and penetrated tropical climes where the evening heat was oppressive. The hot wind and screeching, capricious insects smashed into their faces and naked torsos, and they sweated profusely. Still high on booze and grass, they arrived in El Limón, "a jungle town," where, dead tired, they decided to spend the night. They parked the Ford on the edge of town and settled in as best they could. Neal grabbed a blanket, laid it on the ground, stretched out, and went right to sleep. Frank made himself comfortable in the front of the Ford, while Jack got up on the roof and lay down on the cold, metallic surface. There he had further transcendent, nirvanic sensations:

> For the first time in my life the weather was not something that touched me, that caressed me, froze or sweated me, but became me. The atmosphere and I became the same. (*On the Road*, 294)

Assailed by swarms of furious insects, which pleased rather than disturbed him, he tried to sleep, when a local watchman, flashlight in hand, approached to ask what they were doing. Jack told him they were sleeping. The guard left at once. "Such lovely policemen God hath never wrought in America," Jack concluded. "No suspicions, no fuss, no bother: he was the guardian of the sleeping town, period" (*On the Road*, 294). A little later, still awake, Jack witnessed a scene straight out of Lowry's *Under the Volcano:* a white horse passed quite close to the head of a sleeping Neal, who noticed nothing, then disappeared. "What was this horse? What myth and ghost, what spirit?" wondered Jack Kerouac, eager to transcend apparent reality to another, where some Nahualic power seemed to bubble beneath the strange land that he'd so recently begun to savor.

Before dawn they got into the Ford and followed the road south. They crossed the Moctezuma River and alongside the road observed some girls gesturing at them with rock crystals for sale. The incident somehow resembled a religious encounter. The eyes of the girls "were like the eyes of the Virgin Mother when she was a child. We saw in them the tender and forgiving gaze of Jesus. And stared unflinching into ours. We rubbed our nervous blue eyes and looked again. Still they penetrated us with sorrowful and hypnotic gleam" (*On the Road*, 297).

In a gesture of profound tenderness (the opposite of the rapacious Spanish conquistadors), Cassady traded his wristwatch to one of the girls for a crystal (the watch was obviously worth more). So Christian.

The girls caressed Dean (Neal) and thanked him. Standing between them, he had a look of torment as he scanned the sky for the most distant point, like a prophet.

Back on the highway, ensconced in the beat-up Ford, Jack observed the inhabitants of the Sierra Madre Oriental descending to the towns to join a civilization that would eventually destroy their innocence, unaware that "a bomb had come that could crack all our bridges and roads and reduce them to jumbles" (*On the Road*, 298).

Later he saw "sudden Biblical tree shade" and shepherds' families that evoked Christian symbols and made him rouse Neal from slumber: "Man, man, wake up and see the shepherds, wake up and see the golden world that Jesus came from, with your own eyes you can tell!" (*On the Road*, 298).

Kerouac missed no opportunity to describe Mexico in religious terms. In the evening, after a journey of almost two thousand miles from Denver in which they had penetrated "these vast and Biblical areas of the world," the Ford T entered Mexico City via Avenida Insurgentes to Paseo de la Reforma, submerging into an asphalt sea, where the rugged innocence of Mexico was garbed in noise, traffic, and chaos. Rather than being annoyed by these things, Neal and Jack felt elated:

> Then the city roared in and suddenly we were passing crowded cafés and theaters and many lights. Newsboys yelled at us. Mechanics slouched by, barefoot, with wrenches and rags. Mad barefoot Indian drivers cut across us and surrounded us and tooted and made frantic traffic. The noise was incredible. (*On the Road*, 300)

Neal was in his element: extreme commotion. He wanted to be part of it. "This is traffic I've always dreamed of," he shouted as he drove, dribbling around cars driven by Indians who showed not the slightest respect for traffic regulations. He was glad to be immersed in this hitherto unknown city where speed and daring were the behavioral parameters of its inhabitants, who in 1950 numbered barely two million.

For his part, Jack observed and recorded the new reality that streamed in front of his writer's eye, noting the details, taking the city's pulse as a doctor checks his patient before an operation. And strangely enough, from the instant Jack stepped on Mexican ground, he maintained an unwavering respect for the country that inspired him to religious visions, metaphysical otherness, and commiseration, even as he witnessed its sordidness and monstrous, malodorous filth. Kerouac found Mexico mysterious, spiritually dense, chilling, and quite compassionate (most likely he was projecting his victim's complex, his fears and vulnerabilities on the Mexican personality). As a result, nowhere in his correspondence or in any of his writings did he ever complain about this Indian land. Not a single insult or outburst, even in passing, nothing that might wound the dignity that he believed Mexico to inspire in him. Kerouac never so much as dented the quasi-sacred image he held of this country to the south. There was definitely something Christian about his interpretation of Mexico, which he hoped sprang from his heart rather than his head or liver. Few foreign authors who traveled to Mexico during the twentieth century held such a pious attitude toward this often false friend of a country, which generally held them in warm embrace only to turn around and kick them in the ass when they least expected it.

But for the moment, the traffic of Mexico City was irresistibly fun and exciting, a total joyride, and the three gringos in the 1937 Ford T—urbanites, after all—plunged headlong into the choppy and, to them, unfamiliar waters of the capital.

Neal hurled the vehicle into the traffic and played around with everyone. "He drove like an Indian." The bus drivers were barefoot and dirty, and they swore. They wore T-shirts and hunched behind huge steering wheels, with glittering religious icons hanging over the dashboard. The buses had brown and green lights and the dark faces of the passengers sitting on wooden benches could be glimpsed within.

It bears repeating that the term "Indian," as used by the innocent and well-intentioned Jack, had more of a racial than cultural connotation, and he never used it in a pejorative sense, as do most Mexican mestizos, for whom the term *indio* is a highly derogatory adjective. For Kerouac, any dark-skinned Mexican, whether purely indigenous or mestizo, was an Indian. To say that Neal "drove like an Indian" through the chaotic streets of Mexico City meant only that he enjoyed it tremendously.

That day, before they arrived at the Burroughses' home in the Roma district, intent on having "the great American drinking night," a fellahin night at the end of the road in this "oriental country," as Kerouac quoted Burroughs saying, they explored the lower depths around the perimeter of the city center. The strange, murky odors they breathed in reminded them of the jungles they'd just left. They discovered "beautiful Latin whores," as gorgeous as Hedy Lamarr with the resplendent gazes of Madonnas. They went into nightclubs where music came out of dilapidated jukeboxes and underage women charged a penny a dance, thigh to thigh, crotch rubbing included. One cent! In other words, nothing for Jack, Frank, or Neal, who was spellbound. Seeing Neal, dubbing him the king of friends, Jack couldn't help but make genealogical and cultural references to his country:

> Cody [Neal] was out of his mind, he darted between legs, he popped up like . . . a pop cork from shoulders, he pleaded with my ear: "I've never, I never knew, anything like this!!!" The American Irish pioneer in him was mourning the loss of home, he realized he never had one. (*Visions of Cody*, 386)

Another use that Mexico had for Jack was to help him understand, from afar, a lost America, the one that had seduced and deceived Walt Whitman.

Following this nocturnal voyage through the concrete, during which Jack sensed a torrid Mexico of concealed symbols, which fascinated him and served as fodder for his books, they finally arrived at the home of William S. Burroughs and Joan Vollmer, their former partners in crime. Bill and Joan were renting a small apartment at 37 Cerrada de Medellín (now José Alvarado) in the rundown and increasingly plebeian Roma district, right behind the all-American Sears Roebuck, which, thanks to the modernization campaign of the Miguel Alemán government, had opened its doors in 1947. It wasn't far from the Romita neighborhood, the working-class backdrop for *Los Olvidados*, Luis Buñuel's best Mexican film, which he had just finished shooting. Since the recent arrivals wouldn't fit in the Burroughs's flat, Jack, Neal, and Frank rented the neighboring apartment.

The Burroughses lived with Julie, Joan's six-year-old daughter, and William S. Burroughs III, Billy, the three-year-old son of Joan and William. Ten months earlier, near New Orleans, the Louisiana police had arrested Burroughs for dealing drugs. After his release on bail, awaiting a trial in which he'd likely be convicted, Burroughs followed his lawyer's advice and left the country, settling in Mexico City with Joan and the kids in October 1949.

Joan and Bill had a most unusual relationship. Joan, immersed in a lethal, self-destructive cycle, consumed enormous quantities of tequila and Benzedrine. At age twenty-six, she showed signs of polio in her leg, and her general physical appearance, so youthful and hearty just a short time earlier, had begun to fade irreversibly. Burroughs, at age thirty-six, was addicted to opiates and alcohol and had sex with young men. He had not yet begun to write seriously.

Arriving at Joan and Bill's flat, Jack fell ill. Fever wracked his body, as he sweated out copious toxins. The doctor diagnosed dysentery, prescribed medicine, and advised him to stay in bed. (Thirty-six years earlier, Jack London had also contracted dysentery, in Veracruz.) Not a week passed before Neal went to a prostrate, feverish Jack to announce that he was returning to the United States. Aside from having another road adventure, Neal used the opportunity of his visit to Mexico to file for divorce from his first wife, Carolyn, who lived in San Francisco, so he could marry his new girlfriend, Diane, in New York. Jack, in a dreamy stupor, watched him go. Neal furtively pulled a few bucks from Jack's and Frank's wallets and got into the Ford T, leaving a stricken Jack behind. Jack felt hurt by his friend's abandonment, not to mention his extortionate tactics, but then again indulged the dizzying odysseys of his American hero and forgave him his failure to come through. Frank, for his part, enrolled at Mexico City College and took courses in literature and dramatic arts. When Neal got to Gregoria, he made a quick visit to Victor, his friend from Tamaulipas, then crossed the border. The Ford broke down around a Louisiana lake and he ditched it. Diane sent him a plane ticket so he could fly to New York. Right after his arrival, they got engaged. But within three weeks' time, Neal could no longer take married life, sent his new, now pregnant bride packing, and caught a bus to San Francisco. There he went running back to his ex, Carolyn, with whom he resumed an intense relationship of several years, which produced three children. So it went with the hero of Jack Kerouac's novels.

After recovering, Jack joined Burroughs on an urban tour of the bars of the Roma and Dolores districts. They drank, smoked Rialtos (at thirty-five centavos a pack), ate at the Viennese Kuku, discussed political issues such as the Korean War, which they both criticized. At home Jack listened intently to the fairy tales that Billy told him. Once in a while he went into the Balmori cinema—at Álvaro Obregón and Orizaba in the Roma district—where he saw *Fantomas* with Simone Signoret and Marcel Herrand—or the Chapultepec, where he enjoyed *L'idiot* with Gérard Philipe. He also started drinking and smoking marijuana obsessively, leading a relentlessly alcoholic, cannabinoid life until his departure in early September. And to intensify his mystical experiences, Jack prayed every morning. Although it was his first trip to Mexico, he did no writing of any kind, unlike on his subsequent visits there. Instead, he was doing mental calisthenics so that he could focus on his chief literary work, *On the Road*, when he got back to New York.

Jack and Burroughs went to the Plaza México bullring (not the Toreo de la Condesa, the bullfighting center of the capital until 1946, which was at the corner of Calle Durango and Oaxaca) to see their first *novillada*, which featured the matadors Fernando de los Reyes, El Callao, Ramón Ortega, and Humberto Moro. Jack was disgusted. The brutal ritual deeply offended his Franciscan sensibility and ecumenical love, which extended to animal species . . . unlike the less sensitive Burroughs, who liked his "spectacles brutal, bloody, and degrading":

> He still wasn't dead, an extra idiot rushed out and knifed him with a wren-like dagger in the neck nerve and still the bull dug the sides of his poor mouth in the sand and chewed old blood.—His eyes! O his eyes!—Idiots sniggered because the dagger did this, as though it would not.—A team of hysterical horses were rushed out to chain and drag the bull away, they galloped off but the chain broke and the bull slid in the dust like a dead fly kicked unconsciously by a foot. Ole! Girls throwing flowers at the animal-murder in the fine britches. And I saw how everybody dies and nobody's going to care, I felt how awful it is to live just so you can die like a bull trapped in a screaming human ring. (*Lonesome Traveler*, 32)

His response to the spectacle was not unlike that of Kate, the Irish lady of D. H. Lawrence's *The Plumed Serpent*. On witnessing a bullfight in Mexico City, she went running out of the ring, sickened by the savage spectacle. Following her tumultuous departure, Lawrence declared: "Kate felt that bitter hopelessness that comes over people who know Mexico well. A bitter barren hopelessness." Kerouac would never subscribe to such a notion, considering it overly harsh and reproachful to a country that, rather than disapproval, merited compassion and even gratitude.

In a letter to his friend in New York, the writer John Clellon Holmes, Jack—who had smoked marijuana before going into the bullring—railed against the bullfighting mania of Hemingway and related that, after leaving the arena, he went through a neighborhood of stone houses by a stream that evoked the Ganges. Afterward, sitting on a pile of bricks, he had a vision of God—later "the Great Walking Saint of *On the Road*," an itinerant, visionary being who roamed in penance all over America, proclaiming love, imparting justice, and eliminating the suffering of others. This beatific image somewhat made up for the sensation of brutality he'd experienced in the bullring. But as much as the bullfights disgusted him, he maintained respect for Mexico and never criticized it harshly. Jack forgave Mexico its sins. The evil that he saw in it was not caused by any community of men and women called Mexico but by evil itself, through its agents. Evil was a metahistorical phenomenon. That said, Jack decided to leave Mexico after this experience, and at the beginning of September caught a bus to New York, by himself.

On his first journey to Mexico, Jack Kerouac was truly amazed. Despite its sordidness, he believed he'd found a magical-mystical life spirit in this fellahin land, something he'd never witnessed in his own country. He made almost everything he saw and experienced into something holy: the children, the women, the landscapes, the music, the social environment. Obviously, Jack Kerouac the writer had a tendency to embellish a country that he *wanted* to make magic from the outset, as much as he was marked by its coarseness and cruelty. But like an only child conjuring up an invisible friend, Kerouac invented a *virtual* Mexico that was golden, mysterious, and spiritual. Its symbols lodged in his imagination to compensate for his existential emptiness and imaginatively reaffirmed his spiritual quest and disgust with American civilization.

In fact, I don't even know what I was . . . In any case,

a wondrous mess of contradictions . . . but more fit for

Holy Russia of 19th Century than for this modern

America of crew cuts and sullen faces in Pontiacs.

—JACK KEROUAC, *Desolation Angels*

Returning from Mexico, the first thing Jack Kerouac did was cuddle up to his mom. His Oedipally troubled relationship with Memère remained laden with emotional ambivalence. Alternately loving and hating, mutually supportive and hostile, it bred unhealthy bonds of codependence and murky invisible ties, which the weak but not obtuse Jack never wanted but couldn't quite sever.

Around that time Jack met Joan Haverty, a girl from Albany who would become his second wife. Twenty years old, fine-featured, taller than he was, prim and elegant, she lived next door to Lucien Carr. In November 1950, a few weeks after meeting, they got married on a whim and went to live with Memère in Richmond. The mother-in-law/wife/son/husband quatrain didn't work out very well: Jack's overprotective mother obstructed the couple's relationship, and it got on Joan's nerves. In desperation, she shut herself in her room and stopped eating to protest the insufferable situation. She finally convinced Kerouac to leave his mother, and in March 1951 the couple moved to 454 West 20th Street. There they followed the marital template where the woman obeys and serves the man, though Joan, not Jack, was the breadwinner. Jack did not want his mate to compete intellectually, and as his literary work was his top priority, he sat in front of a typewriter while Joan was laboring in a warehouse. This time he was working up a book that would bear his imprint. So he wouldn't lose his train of thought inserting page after page into the typewriter, he took some six-meter strips of Japanese paper and pasted them together to make a scroll long enough to contain a single paragraph of 175,000 words with no commas and few periods, written over a period of three weeks. This turned out to be the most important and enduring novel of his generation: *On the Road*.

But as this creator of vital literature was being born, his marriage was irreparably expiring after just a few months. As with his first wife, Jack's marriage to Joan never really worked. Although on a moral level he believed in the family, he was too individualistic, irascible, demanding, and dismissive of women's intellectual capacities to share his destiny with a wife. Like Jean-Jacques Rousseau, he wanted a maid/lover, not a wife, a sidekick, not a companion. But unlike the Genevese philosopher, Jack couldn't even deal with this sort of woman. In mid-1951, Joan brought some news that hit Jack like an H-bomb: "I'm pregnant." He was infuriated by the news. He wanted children, but not then and there. He accused her of infidelity—he sometimes found her at home with other men—denied paternity of the baby, and despite his Catholicism wanted her to abort. An indignant Joan went to her mother's place in Albany. Jack —about to go to Mexico with Allen Ginsberg and Lucien Carr— instead ran off to North Carolina to find Memère at the home of his sister Nin. He killed time there kidding around with his nephew Paul and recovering from a devastating and highly psychosomatic case of phlebitis.

In Carolina he got a letter from Ginsberg saying that the editors had not accepted the manuscript for *On the Road* as it stood but proposed a set of revisions that would need to be made before it could be published. Jack accepted and went to New York, phlebitis and all, to red-pencil the original manuscript while reading and studying Dostoyevsky, Blake, Whitman, Lawrence, Flaubert, and Melville and listening to baseball games on the radio. Not far away, in Albany, Joan was awaiting the birth of their child and threatening to sue Jack if he didn't support her financially. Jack played the victim and began drinking heavily, writing after hours, and taking lengthy walks through the streets of the world's most fascinating and reviled city.

True to her word, Joan obtained a court order against him. A stunned Jack sent her five dollars a week for one month. Then he got on a bus and fled to San Pedro, California, thinking he would board the *President Harding* and sail around the world. Some getaway, Jack. But in the end, he wasn't hired and he went to San Francisco to stay with Neal and Carolyn Cassady. Neal and Jack went on endless binges fueled by alcohol, cannabis, and amphetamines, tumultuous all-nighters with multiple prostitutes, all under the angry eye of Carolyn, who'd had it with her crazed and centrifugal husband. Until the inevitable happened: a sexual encounter between Jack and Carolyn that Neal tolerated and even encouraged. Rather than offending him, the affair seemed to excite him and bolster his self-image as a tough dude. Deep down he knew that Jack was not a competent sexual rival. Granting his wife to his friend only exalted his powers of virility. In doing so, Neal was trying to compensate for the intellectual and literary inferiority that he felt toward Jack without admitting it. Through it all, three thousand miles from New York, Jack kept on writing, never mind Joan and the imminent birth of their child.

Neither family, nor women, nor friendships, nor binges, nor whiskey, nor potential children, nor even his mother meant that much to him. What most mattered to Jack in life was writing. And in San Francisco, where he'd attempted unsuccessfully to join the merchant marine, he did it compulsively. At the Cassadys' place, he recorded all the conversations and kidding around, then edited and compiled them for use in his books. On the street he took notes and jotted down observations about anything that might yield valuable grist for his literary mill, from seeing Joan Crawford being filmed on the street in *Sudden Fear* to chatting with Billie Holiday in a bar to following the route of a drunken panhandler. All this scribbling would eventually become a book that he later christened *Visions of Cody*, a sort of paraphrase, or version II, of *On the Road*, written in a freewheeling, experimental style.

During that time, Philip Lamantia, a poet friend of Sicilian heritage whom Jack knew from New York, offered him and Neal some peyote buttons that he'd brought from San Luis Potosí. Jack took them twice. The first time he had a revelatory experience of his own death; the second he slept for twelve hours and had musical dreams. There was no news from his second wife, and Jack felt content there in San Francisco.

But life did not forgive his sins and soon bad news arrived as several publishers gave *On the Road* the thumbs-down. Those that accepted it, like Ace Books where Carl Solomon worked (Ginsberg dedicated his poem *Howl* to Solomon a short time after), requested changes that Kerouac flatly refused to make. The book languished in a drawer for five years before being published. It seemed there would never be a dearth of obtuse editors or abandoned wives waiting in ambush: in February 1952, Joan gave birth to a daughter, Janet Michelle, and as there was no sign of Jack, she went to the police to report the irresponsibility of the innocent creature's father. The police began casing people and places close to Jack, who upon learning of the stakeout figured he would never go back to New York.

Meanwhile, the Neal–Jack pact soured, not because of Carolyn but owing to a string of misunderstandings, petty jealousies, everyday minutiae, and recurrent frictions, which spurred verbal skirmishes, swearing, and shouting matches. Neither could take it any longer; they needed to come down off each other. In late August the Cassadys decided to visit Carolyn's parents in Tennessee. On board a '50 Chevy with no backseat, Jack, Carolyn, and the little baby did their best to accommodate themselves on a mat. In front, the two girls held on to their seats in terror alongside their dad, as he gunned the Chevy down the road. Jack bounced all the way to Nogales.

Disgusted with his best friend, unwilling to recognize his own daughter, hounded by the police, disappointed to see what was perhaps his best book go unpublished, fed up and frustrated and in a generally irritable state of mind, Kerouac figured it wouldn't be a bad idea to go to Mexico, visit Burroughs—lift the hood, and change the oil. Without further ado, he crossed the border and again trod upon the magical Mexican earth to feast on images of innocence and mystery.

THIS LAND IS OUR LAND

In 1901, after six months living in Mexico, a young, nearly broke Englishman arrived in Ciudad Juárez, Chihuahua, aiming to skip across the border to Texas. Aleister Crowley. Magician, occultist, poet, heroin addict, hierophant of cryptic sects, sexual sorcerer, twentieth-century visionary, he remained unrecognized by the stuffy, myopic institutionalized intellectuals of the world. On the threshold to the north, Crowley told how he felt in his *Autohagiography:*

> Coming straight from the quiet civilization of Mexico it was a terrible shock to find myself in touch with the coarse and brutal barbarism of Texas. There are many unpleasant sides of life which

cannot be avoided without shirking reality altogether; but in the United States they were naked and horrible. (Crowley, *The Confessions of Aleister Crowley*, 222)

Although he was going in the opposite direction, Jack Kerouac had something similar in mind as he moved from Nogales, Arizona, to Nogales, Sonora:

When you go across the border at Nogales Arizona some very severe looking American guards, some of them pasty faced with sinister steelrim spectacles go scrounging through all your beat baggage for signs of the scorpions of scofflaw . . . But the moment you cross the little wire gate and you're in Mexico, you feel like you just sneaked out of school when you told the teacher you were sick and she told you you could go home, 2 o'clock in the afternoon. You feel as though you just come home from Sunday morning church and you take off your suit and slip into your soft worn smooth cool overalls, to play . . . in fact the further you go away from the border, and deeper down, the finer it is, as though the influence of civilization hung over the border like a cloud. (*Lonesome Traveler*, 21)

In Jack's mind, Mexico seemed once again like a blessing gilded with smiles, warmth, jubilant faces, without a trace of artificiality. Jack said that he felt good in this Tierra Pura. Mexico continued to be radically different from his own hypercivilized country, where average Americans, steeped in the conventional wisdom, could not help but prejudge their southern neighbor. "There is no 'violence' in Mexico," wrote Jack, "that was all a lot of bull written up by Hollywood writers or writers who went to Mexico to 'be violent.'" As he had two years before, Jack praised and defended the country's idiosyncrasies, which kept him from losing faith in the human race.

Once in Nogales, Sonora, Jack, hoping to save his pesos, hopped a chicken bus going south. His plan was to see Burroughs, who now lived alone at 210 Calle Orizaba in Mexico City.

The big bus was old and dilapidated, with wooden seats. Passengers in rebozos and straw sombreros boarded with their goats, pigs, and chickens, while children rode on the roof or sat on the rear fender, singing and shouting.

At Guaymas, he met a young "hipcat," twenty-five-year-old Enrique, with whom he hit it off immediately. Enrique was carrying a sort of handmade radio case that he used *pour cacher la merde*, that is, to hide the marijuana they bought on arriving in Culiacán, "near the opium center of the world," as Jack put it. Together with his Mexican Cicerone, he sat among the cactuses behind bus stations to smoke as they contemplated the arid plains under tremendous heat. Enrique was traveling with his younger brother Gerardo, whom he would not let smoke grass because it was "bad for the eyesight and bad for the law." As they stopped in Navojoa and passed through Los Mochis, Mexico raised its unavoidably harsh and sordid head:

> Strange towns like Navojoa, where I took a walk by myself and saw, in the market outdoor affair, a butcher standing in front of a pile of lousy beef for sale, flies swarming all over it while mangy skinny fellaheen dogs, scrounged around under the table—and towns like Los Mochis (The Flies) where we sat drinking Orange

Crush like grandees at sticky little tables, where the day's headline in the Los Mochis newspaper told of a midnight gun duel between the Chief of Police and the Mayor—it was all over town, some excitement in the white alleys—both of them with revolvers on their hips, bang, blam, right in the muddy street outside the cantina. (*Lonesome Traveler*, 27).

In the stations Kerouac ate meat and tortillas "in African huts," surrounded by pigs that brushed their legs. They drank maguey sap thinking it was pulque, "the greatest drink in the world," and ate mangoes, which he had never tried before. While he rode in the back of the bus, drinking mezcal, listening to his Mexican friends sing *rancheras* like a cackling lament, he himself sang bop versions of tunes like "Scrapple from the Apple," and Johnny Carisi's "Israel" to them. By midnight they were in Culiacán, not far from the Tropic of Cancer, and the three cats silently made their way to a group of huts made of branches. Enrique rapped at the door of one of them. It was opened by a white-skinned Indian, a hero of fellahin Mexico. He had a huge sombrero, a disdainful air, and his face reminded Jack of his New York junkie pal Herbert Huncke. They went inside. Sitting on the bed was the hieratic wife of the cranky host; at the edge of the bed was a goateed fellow, his eyes drooping from opium; on the floor, submerged in a deep dream, a soldier who had consumed opium and booze was coughing loudly:

> I sat on the bed, Enrique, he squatted on floor, Big Girardo stood
> in the corner like a statue; the host, scornful, made several angry
> remarks; I translated one of them, "Is this Americano following me

from America?" He had once gone to America, to L.A., for maybe twelve hours, and someone rushed . . . (Charters, *Kerouac: Selected Letters, Volume 1*, 347)

In his nationalistic paranoia, the house owner imagined that our unsuspecting, benevolent Jack was an FBI agent carrying an extradition order in his pocket. The host showed the Yankee spy the scars on his neck as irrefutable evidence of American aggression. Later he took out a small black ball, which Jack recognized as opium. This made the man smile, his paranoia now diminished to the point that he forgot all about his antagonism toward the gringo. He grabbed the opium, powdered and sprinkled it on a previously made joint, and offered it to those present. Once he was stoned, the now relaxed host took out a plaster phallus that he himself had sculpted and proceeded to deliver a vehemently pro-indigenous screed. "The land is ours," he said, meaning that the rightful owners of North and South America were the Indians. The speech sounded okay to Jack. Hearing it affirmed his favorable view toward the universal Indian race. At the conclusion of his speech the Mexican delivered a *finale con brio:*

> Is in the rib of mountains of the big plateau! the golds of war are buried deep! the caves bleed! we'll take the snake out of the woods! we'll tear the wings off the great bird! we shall live in the iron houses overturned in fields of rags! (*Lonesome Traveler*, 24)

Now possessed of the divine wisdom of opium, as Jack tells it, he understood everything perfectly, both the language and the message. Finally, the guests bedded down for the night in an adjacent hut, property of the Saint of Opium. The next day, Jack got up and witnessed a daybreaking fellahin scene:

> . . . it was a drowsy sweet little grass hut village with lovely brown maids carrying jugs of water from the main well on their shoulders—smoke of tortillas rose among the trees—dogs barked, children played, and as I say our host was up and splitting twigs with a spear, by throwing the spear to the ground, neatly parting the twigs (or thin boughs) clean in half, an amazing sight. (*Lonesome Traveler*, 28)

Then he attended to nature's call, crouching over a rock, in full view of everyone, yet no one snickered or paid any mind as the gringo defecated in front of the entire community. Shortly before he departed, Jack bought two ounces of marijuana from his host for three dollars, and as the man rolled up a few morning joints that everyone commenced to smoke, some soldiers accompanied by a few police "with sad eyes" entered the hut. Jack thought they were going to arrest everyone, but the calm Enrique told him they just wanted some grass for their own personal use. Which they were given. Jack, hung over as a used syringe, observed as the guardians of public order lay there, rolled their joints, and smoked them calmly. Later, they brought him a spicy broth to relieve his hangover, which "made me gasp, cough and sneeze, and instantly I felt better." After saying good-bye, Jack, Enrique, and Gerardo went to a church and prayed. They then caught a bus to Mazatlán, another city that struck Jack as African, where they swam in the ocean and spent the night at the home of a woman who charged them ten pesos, dinner included. While they were at the beach, swimming in their skivvies, Jack's beatific pH rose and he experienced yet another Mexican epiphany: It "was one of the great mystic rippling moments of my life—I saw right then that Enrique was great and that the Indian, the Mexican is great, straight, simple and perfect." Dream on, Jackie.

They were still dozing when their bus reached Mexico City the next day. Upon arriving, Enrique asked Jack if he could spend the night at the Burroughses' home. Jack, "for obvious reasons," didn't want to, and the three shared a room at a skid-row hotel. When they got up, Enrique, who had to get to Veracruz, asked Jack to join him. But Jack stayed in the capital with the more grounded Burroughs, who later warned him: "You shouldn't hang around with these Mexicans, they're all a bunch of con men." Hearing this, Jack shook his head and put away the rabbit's foot that Enrique had given him.

With his rucksack hanging off his shoulder, his shoes covered with "the dust of great Mexico," he made for 210 Orizaba in the Roma district. Upon entering (it was a Saturday), he saw some women making tortillas on heated *comales*. He heard Pérez Prado mambos on the radio and saw a bunch of kids frolicking in the courtyard. The place was on a small cul-de-sac with two tiny central courtyards, slapped up in the 1930s without any regard for taste—a residential shoebox designed to house low-income families, the opposite of the fabulous Porfirio Díaz–era residences constructed in the Roma district in the early twentieth century. The inappropriate Mexican Revolution ushered in a prosaic regime whose ideological surname was Vulgarity, infecting even the once majestic Roma district. But neither Kerouac nor Burroughs cared about any of that. When traveling, they sought neither luxury nor comfort; it was the interior journey that concerned them.

Burroughs had moved to 210 Orizaba, apartment 5, with Joan and the children in mid-1951. The Joan–William relationship was in an obvious state of decline. Burroughs had a lover on the side, a little gringo by the name of Lewis Marker. Joan knew about it but had no complaint. With all the substances she consumed, she rarely reproached Burroughs for his addictions; she herself was heavily addicted to amphetamines and alcohol. They generally tolerated each other's excesses. Joan showed inexorable signs of self-destruction. The polio that afflicted one of her legs was worsening and her once radiant beauty was brutally dissipating. On the afternoon of September 6, 1951, Burroughs (who had just got back from a trip to South America with Marker) and Joan went to apartment 10 at 122 Monterrey, the home of John Healy, an American friend and owner of the Bounty Bar, on the ground floor of the same building. Burroughs's nubile lover Marker and his friend Eddie Woods were at the apartment. As Burroughs tells it, he had gone to Healy's place to sell a pistol to an acquaintance who never showed up. While they were waiting for him, the four drank gin and rum. No one was really drunk. Suddenly Joan insisted that Burroughs demonstrate his marksmanship. She got up and placed her half-full glass upon her head, then moved to a spot three meters away from the expert marksman. Burroughs pointed and fired. Joan fell to the floor.

Everyone thought she was joking. But Joan did not move. Burroughs approached her, saw the blood trickling on the floor, then started wailing. William Tell had missed the apple.

Joan died shortly afterward and Burroughs was sent to Lecumberri prison. But with the brilliant legal support of the crooked, crafty, and utterly Mexican Bernabé Jurado, he got out on conditional bail in under two weeks, thanks to numerous surreptitious bribes. Corruption is as reprehensible as it is convenient, a practical way around bureaucratic hassles. Julie went to live with her maternal grandparents in Albany, Billy with his father's parents in St. Louis. Burroughs was obliged to stay in Mexico City until the definitive trial, and he had to sign in every Monday at Lecumberri. Since he could not leave Mexico City, he remained at 210 Orizaba and for the first time in his life began to write seriously. As Burroughs told it, Joan's death fatally condemned him to become a writer.

Eight months after those events, the knuckles of Jack Kerouac's right hand rapped on the metal door of Burroughs's apartment. "Bill was like a mad genius in littered rooms when I walked in," Jack related. "He was writing. He looked wild, but his eyes innocent and blue and beautiful."

At the outset, Kerouac and Burroughs happily shared their Mexico City rendezvous. Along with a hophead pal of Burroughs, David Tesorero, and his also addicted wife, Esperanza Villanueva (later to become Jack's Buddhistic lover), they went to Tenancingo for target practice (Burroughs practiced shooting until the end of his days). They also walked in the mountains and canyons where they enjoyed a "Biblical Day and Fellaheen afternoon," with Jack washing his feet in the river as a form of ablution, a clearly mystical ritual. They went to see the Ballet Folklórico and relaxed at Turkish baths, and Jack slept with a large-breasted American woman and "a splendid mex whore." (They found prostitutes on Calle Órgano in the center of town.) On one occasion they went to the pyramids of Teotihuacán, where Burroughs, upon encountering certain killer arachnids, asserted his misogynistic streak:

> [He] said to me "Wanta see a scorpion, boy?" and lifted up a rock—There sat a female scorpion beside the skeleton of its mate, which it had eaten—Yelling "Yaaaah!" [he] lifted a huge rock and smashed it down on the whole scene (and . . . I had to agree with him that time). (*Desolation Angels*, 273)

Both wrote. Jack finished the manuscript of *Visions of Cody* and Burroughs made progress on his Mexican novel, *Queer*. They also took strolls in Chapultepec Park. It was there, Burroughs relates, that Kerouac suggested he write a book and call it "Naked Lunch." And what better place to improve his marksmanship!

> We are sitting on the edge of the lake with tacos and bottles of beer . . . "'Naked Lunch' is the only title," Jack said. I pointed to the vultures . . . Whipping out my pearlhandled .45, I killed six of them in showers of black feathers. (Burroughs, *The Adding Machine*, 178)

They also welcomed various visiting hipsters, all American, among them Wig, a saxophone player whom Jack had met in San

Francisco, who came looking for Burroughs to get drugs and loaned them a record player and LPs by Stan Getz, Bengt Hallberg, Lars Guillin, Charlie Parker, and Miles Davis, which Kerouac listened to over and over. Twice Jack took peyote with Burroughs and his American pals. During the first trip, he went running to Plaza Luis Cabrera (at the corner of Zacatecas and Orizaba) to lie down in the grass and experience the moment intensely. Things did not go so well for him the next time (or for Burroughs):

> Bill and I eat the peyote and get the usual results . . . a charge like a high Benny drive . . . then nausea, and finally the desire to vomit but you can't without great difficulty and if you do anyway you will lose your high at great cost, and for two hours absolute, absolute misery. So Bill gets going on some miserable line . . . he begins with . . . "Ah, I feel awful. I feel worse than if I was suddenly a prisoner in the high Andes." (Charters, *Jack Kerouac: Selected Letters, Volume 1*, 369)

Everything was going fine until Jack started smoking too much marijuana in Bill's home, which greatly upset his host because of the legal risks it posed. Shortly before Jack got to Mexico, the police had arrested Burroughs's old pal Kells Elvins for drug possession, causing him to take even stricter precautionary steps. But the inconsiderate and hardly equable Jack didn't seem to care much about his friend.

After sending Ginsberg the proofed manuscript of *Visions of Cody* for possible publication, Jack wrote a novel in just two months, most of the time sitting in the bathroom stoned on grass. The story, which he titled *Dr. Sax* and subtitled *Faust, Part III*, was a fantasy/parody he'd made up during his teenage years. The eponymous main character was partly based on Burroughs, and Kerouac utilized some Mexican symbols such as the eagle and serpent to assemble his story. The patriotic dual emblem of Mexico seemed anti-Aristotelian, like a symbolic, indissoluble fusion of two icons that complemented rather than excluded each other. At the end of the book, Jack wrote: "Written in Mexico Tenochtitlan, 1952, Ancient Capital of Azteca." Shortly before he finished *Dr. Sax*, Jack went to see *The Wizard of Oz*. The story inspired one of the final scenes with a castle full of snakes, scorpions, gnomes, and a giant arachnid, home of the Wicked Witch of the West.

Although nobody would publish his work, which led him to view editors with a jaundiced eye, Jack never doubted his literary worth or destiny. Not only did he never stop writing but he valued what he'd written, never feigning modesty. From Mexico, he wrote to Ginsberg:

> I know you will love *On the Road*—please read it all, no one has read it all yet . . . Neal had no time, nor Bill. *On the Road* is inspired in its entirety. It is like Ulysses and should be treated with the same gravity. (Charters, *Kerouac: Selected Letters, Volume 1*, 355)

Aside from writing, he cleared his mind and eased his body sleeping with underage prostitutes, who charged him a peso and could always be found on Calle Órgano. In a letter to Neal Cassady he told of his adventures:

. . . there was a 17 year old girl named Luz who induced me to go upstairs with her into a little room with ceiling so low I had to stoop, either that or let my head stand normal between sense-less beams . . . three cots, each surrounded by flimsy blanket curtains, with bouncings . . . then little Luz and I got one of the curtained cots, and she just plopped back there with her legs openbalance relaxed to go (openbalance) and I must confess tho I licked my chops in thought of all this I felt a little like a bas-tard . . . one peso . . . 12 cents . . . but she apparently welcomed all comers (ahem) and in fact seemed to enjoy herself and to think that she was born just to lie there 20, 30 times a night and get her dough with an honest f . . . sc . . . an honest . . . ah, ahem, hey, now, whap . . . (Charters, *Kerouac: Selected Letters, Volume 1*, 359)

In early July, while the Mexican masses were going to the polls to elect the next designated president (exit Miguel Alemán, enter the little professor Ruiz Cortines), Jack was feeling down. He sent letters to the Cassadys—without any reply—telling them of all the things they could afford in Mexico and playing up the mar-velous advantages of living in such an inexpensive country. Myopic editors still considered *On the Road* unpublishable, and *Visions of Cody* was similarly received (even Ginsberg found the latter cum-bersome, with a terrible ending). Jack was jealous of and infuriated by the success of John Clellon Holmes, whose novel *Go* had been accepted for publication while Holmes had been accused of plagia-rizing more than one story. He resigned himself to feeling that his wife would always hate him and that he would never know his daughter; and to top it all off, his relationship with Burroughs was souring.

Although the connection between the two had been congenial and profound, Burroughs grew increasingly exasperated by Jack's total lack of consideration or respect for even the most basic norms of sharing a living space:

> I am not a difficult person to get along with, and I am willing to make every allowance for eccentricities, but I simply cannot get along with Jack . . . He needs analysis. He's so paranoid he thinks everyone else is plotting to take advantage of him so he has to act first in self-defense. For example, when we were out of money and food, I could always rely on him to eat all the food there was if he got the chance. If there were two rolls left, he would always eat both of them. Once he flew into a rage because I had eaten my half of the remaining butter. If anyone asks him to do his part or to share on an equal basis, he thinks they are taking advantage of him. This is insane. (Harris, *The Letters of William S. Burroughs, 1954–1959*, 136)

The situation had become insufferable for both of them, and on July 3, 1952, Burroughs lent Jack twenty dollars to take a bus straight to his sister's home in North Carolina where their mother was then living. A day before leaving, Jack breakfasted on chocolate-covered candy and two beers, entered the church on Santa María la Redonda (now Eje Central Lázaro Cárdenas), and sat below a statue of Christ, whose face brought to his mind a young Robert Mitchum or Enrique stoned on grass (Catholic Jack allowed himself to blaspheme every now and then). Presently, several thoughts paraded through Jack's head, one on the benign effects of the Spanish conquerors' Christianizing mission:

> Here Holy Spain has sent the bloodheart sacrifice of Aztecs of Mexico a picture of tenderness and pity, saying, "This you would do to Man? [referring to the crucifixion of Christ]. I am the Son of Man, I am of Man, I am Man and this you would do to Me, Who Am Man and God—I am God and you would pierce my feet bound together with long nails with big stayfast points on the end slightly blunted by the hammerer's might—this you did to Me, and I preached Love?
>
> "He Preached love, and you would have him bound to a tree and hammered into it with nails, you fools, you should be forgiven." (*Lonesome Traveler*, 34)

Kerouac's fervent, oft-expressed defense of Mexican Indians seemed inconsistent with this patent acknowledgment of Spain's altruistic and civilizing missionary work against the bloodthirsty indigenous culture of old during the years of the Conquest. But given a careful reading, it confirms what's already been said about how Kerouac used the term "Indians" to refer to the dark-skinned Mexicans produced by the hybridization process—without regard to social or cultural differences—rather than to the products of a culture that preserved the original values of pre-Hispanic indigenous people. In any case, Jack was clearly spouting Catholic orthodoxy without thinking through his notion of the Indians or a number of other issues. True to his experiential aesthetic, Jack cherished spontaneity in thought and writing, and wasn't overly concerned with intellectual rigor.

After deliberating over the enormous benefits that the Christian Conquest endowed upon the indigenous barbarians, Jack once again experienced what truly concerned him in life: revelation and divinity:

> I pray on my knees so long, looking up sideways at my Christ, I suddenly wake up in a trance in the church with my knees aching and a sudden realization that I've been listening to a profound buzz in my ears and head and throughout the universe, the intrinsic silence of Purity (which is Divine). I sit in the pew quietly, rubbing my knees, the silence is roaring. (*Lonesome Traveler*, 35)

After the mystical trance subsided, Kerouac went to an altar where the Virgin Mary stood, and as he admired her amid the flowers and colorful adornments, he saw some ragged children playing in the halls of the church. "I get a vision of myself and the two little boys hung up in a great endless universe with nothing overhead and nothing under but Infinite Nothingness, the enormousness of it . . . nothing but emptiness and divine majesty and the silence for the two little boys and me," Kerouac related. Outside the temple, he took one last, fleeting glance at Saint Anthony of Padua. Now that the ecstatic whirlwind had passed, Jack supposed he was completely at peace with himself—"Everything is perfect on the street." Then, feeling pleased with God and Mexico, he continued on his way, like a shadow on the road.

Despite the miraculous revelations, Jack was in a rather disastrous state of mind when he returned to his country. Editors remained indifferent to his books or reluctant to publish them. Even friends like Ginsberg failed to show much enthusiasm for his work. After a brief stay in North Carolina with Memère and his sister, Jack went to see the Cassadys in California. Although lacking the practical sense and skills of Neal, who despite his erratic behavior excelled as a railroad worker, Jack labored there for six months as a railway brakeman. He also renewed his relationship with Carolyn under the eye of Neal, whose confidence wavered as the couple got closer. In fact, the tough guy felt threatened. The once-great friendship succumbed to friction and mutual intolerance, causing Jack to move from the home of his friend and lover to the Hotel Cameo in a rundown section of San Francisco. Carolyn visited him there, though she was spooked by the seediness of the area. Jack could be deeply resentful, particularly toward his friends. In a letter to John Clellon Holmes, he wrote that he'd lost his fondness for Neal, "something insultingly abrupt . . . he has the soul of a baboon." His friend no longer discussed literature, only money. Burroughs he considered a fatuous oldster and Ginsberg's amiability only concealed a scornful nature. Bitterness seemed to ooze from his soul. Deprived even of the chance to be recognized as a writer, seeing his works go unpublished, feeling that his own friends did not fully appreciate his literary output, and scarcely acknowledged as a person—he had no steady mate, he worked on the railroad only to earn a wage, and his wife was still pressing charges against him—Jack unconsciously developed a visceral resentment toward his road buddies to erect an emotional bunker. But despite all the rejections and absence of applause, Jack Kerouac the writer, to our good fortune and perhaps his own misfortune, never backed down.

Besides, Jack's jabs at his friends were temporary, and not long after voicing them he began to see Neal again and made up with Ginsberg via their correspondence. At the start of December 1952, determined to come up for air, Jack quit his job as a brakeman and planned his return to Mexico City. His spirits suddenly revived and he asked Carolyn to join him. Neal didn't like the idea and craftily proposed they make an express trip to the capital in the Ford, ditch it there, buy marijuana, and return as fast as possible. When they got back to San Francisco, he would "permit" Carolyn to catch up with Jack. His innocent pal accepted. During the trip, Neal let Jack drive now and then though he was particular about how his car was handled. Seeing how Jack was about to damage the clutch, he shouted his disapproval, bruising the feelings of his hypersensitive friend.

Unlike on the epic journey they'd made to the magical land of Mexico two-and-a-half years earlier, this time, as a result of hidden feelings, misunderstandings, the nominally practical nature of the itinerary, and the uneasy imposition of the woman they somehow shared, the mystical complicity that had existed between the two friends the first time they trod Mexican soil was gone. Something had broken between Jack and Neal.

When they arrived at 210 Orizaba, apartment 5, in December, Burroughs was stuffing his suitcase with his belongings: needles, flasks, ampoules, photos, books, notebooks. Burroughs was determined to leave Mexico, even though he'd lose his bail, and skip the trial whose date had gotten lost in the thousands of dossiers, procedures, and complications of the loathsome and pachydermic Mexican legal system. Burroughs had had it with Mexico. He could no longer stand to live in a country that would have pleased Franz Kafka. Besides, the police had been hounding him and his opium-using associates David Tesorero and Bill Garver, an old New York friend who'd been living with him for some months. He'd had enough, so he gathered his things and went to Florida. For the first time, Kerouac rented his celebrated rooftop room above Burroughs's apartment. He decorated it with ceramic figures and got busy writing and awaiting Carolyn:

> "I took a little dobe block up on Bill's roof, 2 rooms, lots of sun and
> old Indian women doing the wash. Will stay here awhile even
> though $12 a month is high rent. But perfect place to write, blast,
> think, fresh air, sun, moon, stars, the Roof of the City. All ready
> for your visit, Carolyn . . . Please visit me Carolyn, my little pad is
> all ready . . . come on & get your vacation with me!—We'll have
> wine, tea, 8c oysters at midnight—we'll go dance the Mambo . . ."
> (Charters, *Kerouac: Selected Letters, Volume 1*, 385)

Neal scored some marijuana and hightailed it back to San Francisco in just two days. Alone now, Jack got back to writing at his usual delirious pace. In five days he'd written a novella, in French, in which he and Neal appear as boys along with uncle Bull Ballon (Burroughs), a work he later expanded and titled *Maggie Cassidy*. He also began his *Vanity of Duluoz* and sent John Clellon Holmes several pages on the notion of the Beat Generation, about which Holmes had been writing an article and credited Jack with coining the term. Aside from writing, Jack cooked like a gourmet chef: he fried oysters in butter, ate French bread, and drank imported Chianti. He also took his share of sedatives, Benzedrine, laudanum, and Nescafé. From his time as a brakeman in San Francisco, the railway company owed him thirty dollars, which he'd entrusted Neal with mailing him; otherwise, Carolyn could bring it down with her when she came to Mexico. Neither of those things happened. Neal received the thirty bucks but spent them all, because, as he saw it, Jack had not contributed a cent for gas during the trip. Jack was indignant. In reality, Neal was jealous of his comrade and did everything in his power to deter his beloved Carolyn, who had no will of her own, from traveling by herself to Mexico. And it worked. Carolyn never left San Francisco. She didn't even tell Jack that she wasn't coming. She just never showed up. A little before Christmas, less than three weeks after arriving in Mexico, ensconced in his sad and lonely rooftop room, Jack decided to hitchhike back to the United States. This Mexican jaunt had been short and disheartening. Memère awaited him in New York.

One good thing about Mexico, you just

get high and dig eternity every day.

—JACK KEROUAC, letter to Carolyn Cassady, in Charters,

Jack Kerouac: Selected Letters, Volume 1, 1940–1956

Jack returned to New York in the same deplorable spirits. It was
early 1953. As much as editors said they were interested in his book,
among them the high-profile critic Malcolm Cowley, no one would
actually publish anything. And when John Clellon Holmes received
the not unimpressive sum of twenty thousand dollars for the publication of *Go*—of which Holmes awarded his unknown peer a grand
total of fifty dollars—Kerouac writhed in envy and bitterness, thinking that the quality of Holmes's work was clearly inferior to his
own (history proved him right) and feeling that the editors were
committing a major injustice by passing on it. Unrecognized, his
self-esteem bruised and flat broke, Jack decided to go back to work
as a brakeman for the railway but after a month clashed with his boss
and quit. Later he signed on as a waiter on the *William Carruth*, a
boat that sailed from California to New York with a stop in Panama,
enabling the shattered Jack to get completely smashed, sleep with a

pair of local prostitutes, and appear half-naked with one of them before his enraged superiors who told him off. When the *Carruth* called at the port of New Orleans, Jack flashed an eloquent three-fingered gesture, got paid, and went to New York and his inevitable mother.

Kerouac's readers should be eternally grateful for his total inability to hold a steady job. Literature consumed him to a fatal degree: he simply could not do anything else.

Around that time, Jack, who was drinking and smoking marijuana more heavily than usual, got the idea into his head of going to live in Mexico City for an extended period. But instead of running off to Mexico, he had an affair with one of Ginsberg's women friends by the name of Mardou Fox, as Jack dubbed her literarily. He met her at the Village bar Fugazzi's. Twenty-two years old, black, with fine facial features and a sensual voice, a serious reader, as smart, thought Jack, as Joan Vollmer Burroughs. But even as his ardor for Mardou reached its peak, he never thought of marrying her. What he desired was an out-of-the-ordinary relationship with an out-of-the-ordinary woman. After the dismal experience he'd had with his second wife, the last thing he wanted was to formalize his relationships with women: passion, not convention, with the females. And who better to fit the bill than a black lover with shades of Baudelaire's Juana Duval, Rimbaud's black Tunisians, or Gaugin's Tahitian nymphs? Not a month had passed in their passionate romance when Gregory Corso appeared—the poet was not yet Jack's close friend—and whisked her away. In the end, Mardou opted to stay with Corso. But instead of thrashing the usurper, Jack ran home to Memère, planted himself in front of the typewriter, took a steady stream of Benzedrine, and within seventy-two hours had written a novel on the episode, *The Subterraneans*. It was a brief, distilled Kerouacian gem, in which his spontaneous, boppish prose attained moments of stylistic perfection, and it underlined his ability to save his own life through literature and compensate, if only fleetingly, for his suffering. A refugee from the world of men, Jack could do nothing else.

Here again we must be grateful to Jack Kerouac for his ineptitude in maintaining stable relationships. Thank God he was neither psychoanalyzed nor in some therapy that promised to "cure" him or "straighten him out." Jack never wanted, nor was he able, to swim with the current. Apostle in the art of living, he instead bore a kind of sacrifice, in which the image of the good father, the possessor of two flashy cars in the garage, the hygienic and vivacious wife, the well-groomed children, and the respectable job faded away as the visionary writer forced himself to dwell in life's nether regions, quite unlike the more traveled terrain and therefore irrevocable and perilous. Jack was willing to pay the price. It was his black angel intransigence. So, with a touch of sadness and a bottle of bourbon by his side, he accepted his fate.

Without money or female companionship, without the immediate expectation of seeing his four books published, Jack worked for a spell at the New York Post Office, shared a place with Ginsberg and Burroughs, who was passing through the United States, and one day planted himself on the westbound side of the highway and hitched to San Francisco to see the Cassadys. But his relationship with Neal would never be the same. Both Carolyn and Neal, who had broken his leg in a railway accident and was convalescing, were transfixed by the esoteric ideas of Edgar Cayce, a clairvoyant who enjoyed some fame, and they could not stop talking about him for a minute. Jack was getting sick and tired of Neal going on about Cayce like "Billy Graham in a suit." Once again he moved to a low-rent district of of San Francisco. And to compensate for the impossibility of patching things up with Neal and Carolyn, Jack discovered something that would mark him for life: Buddhism. He steeped himself in writings on the life and ideas of Buddha, and ruminated on the different sutras, so broadening his religious vision that he even criticized Christ. Revitalized within, he wrote a book of poems, *San Francisco Blues*. The first in a series that he would draft over the next few years, it was unrestrained, spontaneous poetry guided by his experiential aesthetic. In April 1954 he returned to New York, his spirit now nourished by new religious proteins, carrying the manuscript of his blues-infused poems.

Now living with Memère in New York, he preached Buddhism to his friends, trying to convince them of the need to detach themselves from their little I's and to keep well away from their mundane ambitions and simply not do anything. Only the hyperactive Jack was himself unable to renounce doing things, much less refrain from pounding away at his typewriter. At his mother's house he worked up a book on Buddhism, *Some of the Dharma*, a *Book of Dreams*, and a science fiction story, *cityCityCITY*.

Far from involving himself in mundane affairs, he went to the other extreme, breaking with his Buddhistic Beat ideals and speaking out in favor of Senator Joseph McCarthy's hysterical brand of anticommunism—a view he never renounced. He now took his fear of the world for granted. Feeling cornered, the supreme prophet of the Beat Generation gradually turned away from the ideals and spirit that he himself had codified in such a visionary manner. With time, Jack became horrified by what his own discoveries and revelations had unleashed on the cultural front. Deep down, he fled fame as much as he sought it. His centripetal tendencies were reinforced by an ever greater consumption of alcohol, marijuana, and Benzedrine, which inflamed his phlebitis. Kerouac never had the stomach for prophethood.

And to make matters worse, he had to appear in court owing to the relentless lawsuits of the tenacious Joan, who persisted in demanding that he take on some responsibility for the upbringing of his daughter. Eugene, Ginsberg's attorney brother, managed to clear him of his paternal obligations for a while, citing an inability to work because of his phlebitis. Seeing the photos of Janet, he had to admit that the girl certainly had his genes. But fatherhood was simply not in the cards for Jack.

Toward the end of 1954, Jack went to North Carolina to be with his family. There he wrote, drank to excess, meditated at night with

Siddhartha Gautama, played with his nephew, and experienced terrible mood swings, which, despite his supposed faith in Buddhism, drove him to consider suicide. Jack was at his wits' end. Then, suddenly, some good news: the magazine *New World Writing* had agreed to publish "Jazz of the Beat Generation," a compilation of excerpts from *On the Road* and *Visions of Cody;* and the *Paris Review* would run his story "The Mexican Girl." But even this development failed to lift his spirits. For the first time in his life, he had the dreadful feeling that not even his long-awaited recognition or much-yearned-for celebrity could do anything to diminish his emotional instability. Nothing could fill his internal hollows. On the contrary, sensing his proximity to fame, he envisioned a precipitous fall and glimpsed another cloud over his brilliant, shell-shocked head. On the verge of a nervous breakdown, exasperated by his sister and brother-in-law, whom he could no longer stand, fed up with the indecisiveness of editors, and ill with phlebitis, Jack decided to head for one of the few corners of the world where he could come up for air: Mexico.

THE SORROW OF JACK KEROUAC

From New York, Jack got a ride to Texas and crossed the border via Laredo. In early August 1955 he arrived in Mexico City and made for his usual crib at apartment 5, 210 Calle Orizaba. It was now occupied by Bill Garver, an acquaintance from his New York days, an opiate addict and an expert in the art of stealing coats, which he pawned to feed his drug habit. In 1952, Garver's father left him a substantial sum of money, enough so that he could give up coat snatching and go to live in Mexico City. There he lived for a few months with Burroughs, who didn't suffer his foolishness for long. When the author of *Naked Lunch* left Mexico, the elderly Garver stayed on in the apartment, happy that he could get a variety of opium derivatives much more easily than in New York and consume them twenty-four hours a day. To kill time, he read volumes of classical history and nineteenth-century French poetry, but his one true passion was to satiate his substance addiction. No sex or anything else: to jab his veins, without the slightest guilt or scruple, was the sole reason for his existence.

Jack now had a new mental accessory: Buddhism, along with the whole megillah of precepts, commandments, prayers, restrictions, and visions. His brand of Buddhism was wrapped up with his highly idiosyncratic Catholic vision of the world. At the start of his fourth stay in Mexico, Jack resided in Garver's apartment, sleeping on the floor. But after a few days he moved up to the roof apartment with the mystical intention of leaving behind worldly matters and living in a state of meditation and solitude. Within his adobe lair he chanted a different sutra every day: Monday, Dana (charity); Tuesday, Sila (spirituality); Wednesday, Ashanti (patience); Thursday, Dhyana (tranquillity); Friday, Prajna (knowledge); Saturday, the conclusion; Sundays he rested. And every day, without fail, he chanted the Diamond Sutra.

Jack was comfortable in his monastic cell despite the fact that there was no electricity and he had to use candles for lighting. He was inches from some obese women who gabbed incessantly while washing piles of clothing in the rooftop basins. The puddly, slippery surface of the rooftop/skylight made him nervous, as he feared the children playing there would tumble down two stories.

Notwithstanding the vows of asceticism and chastity demanded by Buddhism, Jack regularly went down to Garver's and on occasion shot morphine and drank with him. As a result, his phlebitis acted up and he contracted dysentery again. One of the reasons he'd crossed the southern border in the first place was to get his phlebitis cured, because penicillin was much cheaper in Mexico. While he was with Garver, Jack sat in a rocking chair and listened to the superannuated Yankee with his endless diatribes on historical and poetic subjects. At some point Jack began to feel that Garver's words had lost all literal meaning and faded out to become sonic catalysts for a series of poetic spirals that spontaneously lodged in his brain. And so he began to write a series of choruses, infused with the mature Kerouacian aesthetic of impromptu jazz riffs and now Buddhism, which preached the irreversible and infinite continuity of the life force. For Kerouac, Buddhism turned out to be more of a tool for writing than a guide to living. The result was *Mexico City Blues*, a Buddhistic-jazz poem, "the greatest religious poetry I've ever heard," according to Gary Snyder. Paradoxically, the poems only made sporadic mention of Mexico City, and its unmerited title was taken from one of the most horrific, slum-ridden, and antipoetic megacities on the planet simply because it was written there.

While Jack was jazzing up the alphabet, Allen Ginsberg sent him a long poem from San Francisco that he had just finished. After reading it, Jack recognized its explosive power, though he criticized Ginsberg for not being completely faithful to the spontaneity of his inner voice. He also suggested the poem's title, "Howl." Months later, it burst like a multimegaton blast in the USA.

This time—by Buddhist mandate—Jack did not visit the whores on Calle Órgano, and although he masturbated, he was determined not to touch a woman, nor to drink or smoke marijuana, a pledge he obviously could not keep. Nevertheless, it was during this period that he experienced his only Mexican romance. The damsel was named Esperanza Villanueva. Tall, slender, dark, "Indian," as Jack would say, twenty-two years old, a prostitute who went by the name of Saragossa when she was working the streets, according to Jack, or, more likely, Zaragoza.

Here was a latter-day Raskolnikov in jeans infatuated with a streetwalking, long-suffering Mexican Sonia. Esperanza had been the wife of Dave Tesorero, Burroughs's old dealer and shooting-up partner, and later of Garver. "Had been," because Dave died in November 1954. Catholic, a devotee of the Virgin of Guadalupe, irascible, fickle, addicted to opiates, with her eyelids drooping à la Billie Holiday, wearing dark glasses with her pigtails rolled up in back, Esperanza was the proverbial image of pain and self-destruction. In no time she had hooked Buddhist Jack, who desired her sexually but was determined to practice the Buddhist precept of *karuna* (compassion) with her. All of which led Jack, who had met her three years before but had not yet fallen in love with her, to write a novel with Esperanza as the main character: *Tristessa*.

Shortly after arriving in Mexico, right after seeing her, he described his feelings to Ginsberg:

> Old Dave died, a year ago—the
> Old Ike of Bill's book.—His wife
> Is the most beautiful—wow—
> What an Indian and what a
> High priestess Billy Holiday—
> Her name on the street: Saragossa—
> Like Genet Hero name—
> I fell in love with her
> For an afternoon—
> (Charters, *Jack Kerouac:*
> *Selected Letters, Volume 1*, 506)

In Esperanza and the atmosphere that surrounded her Jack saw the proverbial arena of human suffering. Her home was a rooftop hovel of "Blakean adobe" where she lived with her sister Cruz—"a little Indian woman with no chin and bright eyes [who] wears high heel pumps without stockings and battered dresses" in "the poor district of Rome." It had a leaky roof and was inhabited by various animal species that prowled the room: a Chihuahua, a dove, a rooster, a hen, a cat. An image of the Virgin of Guadalupe shone brightly in a corner beside a portrait of the deceased Dave Tesorero, whom Esperanza said she still loved. Together they had made a pilgrimage to Chalma, advancing on their knees toward the patron saint of

Mexican drug addicts and outcasts. Now and then El Indio, a con man who was Esperanza's godfather, went to the sisters' home and shot morphine. "Hm za . . . the Aztec needle in my flesh of flame," he'd shout. The room was always "littered completely and ransacked as by madmen with torn newspapers and the chicken's pecking at the rice and the bits of sandwiches on the floor."

Compassionate observer of this catacomb, this domain of pain and degradation, this eastern-flavored symbol of redemption, Jack exclaimed Buddhistically:

> It's gloom as unpredicted on this earth, I realize all the uncountable manifestations the thinking-mind invents to place wall of horror before its pure perfect realization that there is no wall and no horror just Transcendental Empty Kissable Milk Light of Everlasting Eternity's true and perfectly empty nature. (*Tristessa*, 16)

Esperanza's sordid environment provided Jack with proof of Buddha's first canon: life in this world is suffering. Living with Esperanza and her sister, burrowing into her tiny, fetid catacomb, residing in the Mexico City of 1955 confirmed that linking yourself to the values of the physical and worldly plane of existence meant condemning yourself to eternal suffering. Esperanza was the epitome of human affliction. But Jack also saw the other side of this fatal reality: behind the torment of life there existed the possibility of transcendence, of breaching the barriers imposed by the world, through renouncement and detachment. Prostitute and hysterical morphinomaniac that she was ("she is so high all the time, and sick, shooting ten gramos of morphine per month"), Esperanza represented not just pain and degradation but also—thanks to the religious wisdom Jack believed he possessed—liberation from the burden of human investiture. What's more, Jack tells us in true Dostoyevskian fashion, it is within the murk of one's personal life, in the lowest depths of depravation (he was not referring to sin), that one can see the light of interior liberation. And so, there in Esperanza's sordid enclave they spoke of God and detachment from worldly possessions. "Ees when, cuando, my friend does not pays me back, don I don't care. Because . . . my Lord pay me—and he pay me more . . . ," Esperanza tells Jack, who plays nirvana-like with the rooster, the hen, the dog, and the cat, as he picks up the divine vibrations from the dove upon the window sill impassively observing those around her. Hearing and watching Esperanza, the spellbound Jack said to himself: "I love her, I fall in love with her." Although he wanted to kiss her, he held back, telling himself that she seemed like "a wise woman . . . a divine additional nun [who] will not be cause of further rebirth and will go straight to her God and He will recompense her multibillion-fold in aeons and aeons of dead Karma time." And true to his path of Buddhistic romance, he did not touch her.

But even with his Buddhist goggles on, Jack could not fail to see Esperanza the woman, to observe her marvelous thighs, the way she stripped off her stockings, her lilting walk, and he found her glamorous:

> She is such a beautiful girl, I wonder what all my friends would say back in New York and up in San Francisco, and what would happen down in Nola when you see her cutting down Canal Street

in the hot sun and she has dark glasses and a lazy walk. . . . Her eyes are radiant and shining and her cheek is wet from the mist and her Indian hair is black and cool . . . You picture what a beautiful girl in New York wearing a flowery skirt a la New Look with Dior flat bosomed pink cashmere sweater, and her lips and eyes do the same and do the rest. (*Tristessa*, 10)

As Jack observed Esperanza's sinister vicissitudes and sage attitude, he was essentially projecting his own image upon the woman he said he loved: "How is Jack,—?—" She always asks: "Why are you so sad??— 'Muy dolorosa'" and as though to mean "You are very full of pain," for pain means *dolor*—"I am sad because all la vida es dolorosa" . . .

Esperanza was a female version of Jack: a desperate drug addict, with an ill-magnetized compass, self-destructive, eager for absolutes that might redeem her. Both were pieces that failed to fit into society's puzzle. The only existential difference was that Jack wrote and Esperanza whored, and that she "goes about [her addiction] skinny and carefree, where an American would be gloomy."

One night, after drinking whiskey and Canada Dry and shooting up morphine, Jack left Esperanza's house and delved into the urban tangle of downtown Mexico City. On Calle de Panamá, heart of the Lagunilla district, he saw hundreds of prostitutes lined up on the sidewalks, young men giving them the once over, taxi drivers on the prowl, nasty-looking thieves at work, fat women cooking up pig meat, police passing "idly like figures on little wheel-thucks rolling by invisibly under the sidewalk," gay bars, whoring youths, and mobile food vendors:

I buy stinking livers of sausages chopped in black white onions steaming hot in grease that crackles on the inverted fender of the grill—I munch down on heats and hot-sauce salsas . . . I buy another [taco], further, two of broken cow-meat hacked on the woodblock, head and all it seems, bits of grit and gristle, all mungied together on a mangy tortilla and chewed down with salt, onions, and green leaf . . . (*Tristessa*, 39)

The Mexico that Jack was now witnessing seemed sordid and odoriferous. The lanterns and candles lighting the food stalls, the buses barreling through mud puddles, made a sad spectacle. He arrived at Plaza Garibaldi where a motley mob of musicians and people of every social class crowded around, swilling and singing, while whores clad in yellow strolled by provocatively, and drunks were kicked out of seedy cantinas, landing abruptly on the street. Jack wanted to experience Mexico City's underbelly. He didn't go to posh restaurants or wealthy parts of town, he didn't seek out aseptic artists or well-off people. Decent citizens bored him. He stayed away from sterile nightclubs and reputable theaters, preferring the seamier spots, the filth, the social muck. As Malcolm Lowry, another wingless poet, wrote of Mexico, "the name of this land is hell." Kerouac's fellahin Mexico had lost its happy gloss. The magic he'd experienced on his first visit was now of a thoroughly different kind. Seen up close, face-to-face, Mexico was sinister, though at heart it concealed a profound vein of religious wisdom that demanded Jack's respect and compassion. Even so, in a moment of desperation there on San Juan de Letrán, he lambasted the passersby:

"You're nuts!" (he yelled) to the crowds in English. "You don't know what in a hell you're doing in this eternity bell rope tower swing to the puppeteer of Magadha, Mara the Tempter, insane. . . . And you all eagle and you beagle and you buy—All you bingle you baffle you lie—. . . you don't know that the Lord has arranged everything in sight." "Including your death." (*Tristessa*, 42)

Jack's reproachful words were not so much aimed at the Mexicans but at the whole human race for its inattentiveness, its inability to harmonize with the divine. Still, he saw that Mexico possessed hidden virtues, arcane secrets that could elevate its people to a higher plane, like the secrets Esperanza possessed. Mexico was Esperanza Villanueva, and Esperanza Villanueva was the quintessential human being: pain incarnate and the possibility of transcending it through religion. Jack's attitude toward Esperanza was analogous to that of Raskolnikov, the repentant sinner in *Crime and Punishment*, when he knelt before Sonia—humanity—to beg forgiveness.

Walking along San Juan de Letrán, Jack heard the strains of cha-chas coming out of the late-night bars where people danced the night away. It was raining and Jack ran all the way to the Roma neighborhood. He arrived at Avenida Chapultepec—three blocks from No. 40 Calle Napoles, where at that time another amazing, certainly self-destructive, and still unknown character, Ernesto Che Guevara, was residing with his wife. (Like Jack, Che was a glutton for unpleasant realities.) He walked in front of the Cine México, progressed along the median of Avenida Álvaro Obregón, checked the dark marquee of the Cine Balmori, turned left at Orizaba, passed by La Bella Italia ice-cream parlor, and stopped at Plaza Luis Cabrera. It was two in the morning. Jack was still experiencing the effects of morphine and alcohol. The fountain at the center of the plaza was turned off. "It's the dismal rainy night caught up with me—my hair is dripping water, my shoes are slopping . . ." A block later, on Orizaba, he saw a bakery where he had bought some syrupy donuts before. The journey through the quagmire of human existence was at an end:

> I cross the last street, slow down and relax letting out breath and stumbling on my muscles, now I go in, death or no death, and sleep the sweet sleep of white angels. (*Tristessa*, 46)

Days later, Esperanza visited Jack on his rooftop. In a folksy blend of English and Spanish, she spoke to him anxiously, pacing up and down, without smiling, unable to calm down. Jack heard her without listening to the words. Esperanza broached the subject of friendship and the futility of money. She saw Jack's manuscripts strewn across the floor, pointed to them and told the writer he had a million potential pesos lying there. This shrewd hooker was on to something. Jack smiled and gazed at her legs. Compassion and desire got jumbled in his head and crawled under his skin. But the Buddhist credo won out over the offenses of the flesh: "It's all my own sin if I make a play for her." And he didn't dare even to brush against her. "Leave Tristessa alone," he told himself. He escorted her to a taxi in the middle of the night. As she was going down a metal staircase, Esperanza tripped, letting out a string of curses as she fell. They turned off the street, hailed a taxi on Orizaba, Esperanza got in and left. Bewildered, Jack watched her leave, feeling baffled at having let her go without reaching out physically to his beloved. Was it out of respect for her, for fear of hurting her, to rack up some credit in the Universal Bank of Karma? Not even he knew for sure. Just a year later he went back to see her.

Cloistered once again in his rooftop room, totally breaking his vows of abstinence from substances, with just a tallow candle and his morning prayers for illumination, Jack began to write the first part of *Tristessa*, a true jazz narrative, some of his most Buddhistic writing, a dizzying sax solo in prose with an enormous sonic continuity and impeccable rhythm. Jack should have been a musician. *Tristessa* is the only Beat novel entirely about Mexico, and it deals with some of the ultimate issues facing human beings: God, eternity, pain, reincarnation, religious salvation . . . subjects that Latin American writers and readers don't like to deal with or read about.

Having written a book and a half, had a "Buddhistic" romance, failed in his attempt to cure his phlebitis with penicillin, and disobeyed his own rules about consuming Mary Jane, Jack said goodbye to Garver and left Mexico in mid-September. The Mexico he was leaving seemed seamier now that he'd tasted the bitter honey of its subterranean strata. But it "innocently" yielded enough magical and religious ingredients for him to retain a quasi-luminous image of it:

> You see the Indian ladies in the inscrutable dark of doorways, look-
> ing like holes in the wall not women—their clothes—and you look
> again and see the brave, the noble mujer, the mother, the woman,
> the Virgin Mary of Mexico. (*Tristessa*, 11)

Long live the religious wisdom of our Marías. After several years of contact with this land, Kerouac had finally formed a notion of Mexico. It was like a maguey plant: apparently sinister and aggressive but concealing a secret and redemptive pulp. The poet is a pretender and a fantasist.

Before he departed for the United States, the prophet Jack Kerouac felt that something important was going to befall him and his traveling brethren, that his words and ideas were destined to shatter the earth . . . A few days before taking off, he wrote Ginsberg a letter, and the last line augured the immediate future of their literary generation:

LET'S SHOUT OUR POEMS IN SAN FRANCISCO STREETS
—PREDICT EARTHQUAKES!

5

I'd run across a Saint in Modern Mexico and here I was

fantasizing dreams away about foreordained orders for nothing . . .

—JACK KEROUAC, *Tristessa*

Jack traveled by bus to El Paso, then hitchhiked and took the train to San Francisco, epicenter of American culture and life in the fifties, sixties, and seventies. A countercultural big bang that reverberated all across the planet. Ground zero of the Beat blast, the prodigal, gleeful flower bed of the hippie movement, sanctuary of a magical, divinely feverish brand of rock 'n' roll. But also the place where the Reverend Jim Jones founded his Peoples Temple shortly before downing poison with his almost two thousand followers in Guyana; where the crazed, self-designated Beat Charles Manson ("I'm not a hippie, I was a beatnik before the hippies got started," he said) went on a freakout carving up people at random; and where Patty Hearst was kidnapped by fundamentalist believers in bogus utopias. Jack Kerouac arrived in San Francisco and, together with Ginsberg and a bunch of like-minded poets—Ferlinghetti, Lamantia, Whalen, McClure, Snyder—hatched the Beat literary scene at the famous Six Gallery, where various poets read their irreverent works. Among them was Ginsberg, who in reading *Howl* demonstrated that even in an antipoetic world it was still possible to break open the odd obtuse head.

Still into Buddhism, Jack had a fortuitous encounter with Zen poet Gary Snyder, with whom he discussed, pondered, and unraveled Buddhist sutras. In an initiatory ritual, the two almost reached the summit of the Matterhorn, getting within thirty-five yards of the peak. Jack felt glad to be around his travel buddies. His writings were starting to be published in magazines and Malcolm Cowley promised that *On the Road* would be published by Viking Press. Jack sensed his nearness to fame and recognition, but rather than grounding him in the undesirable world of men, it only exacerbated his centripetal tendencies. He was drinking more, getting increasingly cranky and antisocial, even with his friends, many of whom he was starting to annoy with his outbursts prompted by the ever-present booze. The closer he got to being famous, the more Jack Kerouac soared to rarefied heights.

But he didn't stop writing. It took him two weeks to finish *Visions of Gerard*, an account of his brother, and some very free writing on Buddhism, adding to the pile of unpublished books. Anchorite that he was, Jack had a long-cherished dream of retreating to a place where he could meditate and write in absolute solitude. To that end he sought work as a fire lookout in some mountainous region, and in June 1950 he signed on for a two-month stay at Desolation Peak in Washington's Mount Baker National Reserve. Without any alcohol, marijuana, or amphetamines, hoping to write, meditate, and practice the Taoist philosophy of *wu wei* (nondoing), Jack got on a mule and after a long, winding journey arrived at a cabin on the aforementioned peak. At first he was enthusiastic but before long he got bored and exasperated. He only scribbled in his journal, and apart from the time he spotted a rogue bear from afar, absolutely nothing happened. Neither the forest nor his soul saw the slightest flicker or flame. His work done, he took his pay and caught a bus to San Francisco, where he lived for a spell at the Cassadys' new home, diving into poetry readings and get-togethers with his poet pals, among them Gregory Corso. Toward the end of September, bearing a notebook and a newly sharpened pencil, with a strong desire to drink and "be a man of Tao who watches the clouds and lets history rage beneath," he decided to go it alone to Mexico.

ADIÓS TRISTESSA

From San Francisco he made a stop in Los Angeles, then went to Tucson, where he put his sleeping bag in the desert under a full moon, even though he had enough money to spend the night in a hotel. While he was contemplating the universe and its strange, luminous creations, some police approached this suspicious vagabond. When they asked him what he was doing out in the desert in the middle of the night, Jack answered that he was looking for a little peace. They let him go, without ever comprehending why he'd rather sleep outside than on a soft hotel bed.

In September 1956, Jack caught a bus from Nogales to Mexico

City. Once again he rented the rooftop room at 210 Orizaba where Bill Garver was still living, reading, digressing, and consuming opiates. Jack straightened out his little refuge, bought some candles, and started writing *Desolation Angels*. Sometimes he went downstairs to see Garver, entered his room, which had "a Persian feeling ... of an old Guruish Oriental Minister of the Court ... ," watched him take codeine, listened to him going on about H. G. Wells's *Outline of History* (which Garver knew by heart), the analogous condition of artists and drug addicts, Orphism, Rimbaud, or Mallarmé, or went shopping for provisions at the corner store:

> Then he'd send me on errands: to the corner store for boiled ham, sliced by machine by the Greekish proprietor who was a typical tightfisted middleclass Mexican merchant but sorta liked Old Bull Gaines, called him "Señor Gahr-va" (almost like Sanskrit)—Then I'd have to go traipsing to Sears Roebuck on Insurgentes Street for his weekly *News Report* and *Time Magazine*, which he read from cover to cover in his easy chair, high on morphine ... (*Desolation Angels*, 252)

He and Garver went looking for drugs all over town. Sometimes they'd try a laundromat with a Chinese owner. Garver would ask the man if he had any opium, to which he would invariably respond, "No savvy. No, no, no." "Them Chinese are the most tightlipped junkeys in the world," Garver used to say. Or they'd take a taxi to corruptible drugstores where Jack would get out to buy codeine tablets while Garver and the driver waited in the cab. Then, to throw off the driver, they'd get out a few blocks from 210 Orizaba, sometimes at the corner of Orizaba and Álvaro Obregón in front of the Balmori movie theater, where they'd buy cones or pops at La Heroica, an ice cream cart that worked the corner for forty years.

During those jaunts, Jack again met up with his Buddhistic love, Esperanza Villanueva. Haggard and battered, even more addicted to morphine and sedatives, with a recently developed leg ailment and cysts on her arms, Esperanza seemed to Jack on the verge of self-destruction. Once, while with him at Garver's place without any pills, she had a fit of hysteria and started to break, batter, or hurl every household object until everything was smashed to pieces as she howled and dragged herself across the floor in jolts. The gossipy landladies were "hovering at the door thinking we're beating her up but she's beating us up." She accused Jack of being a lowdown pothead and threw a bottle at him. "I had to struggle with her—Bull and I hid the bread knife under the rug." Garver was so afraid she would kill him that a week earlier he had called the police and an ambulance to take her away but they couldn't manage to do so. The morning after her outburst, Esperanza, "pale and beautiful, no more an Aztec witch," asked them for candy and humble forgiveness.

Days later, Jack set out on a new foray through the sordid, godless hollows of Mexico City. He got into a taxi with Esperanza and Garver, and there in the back seat, as they rode into the center of town, he confessed to Esperanza that he loved her. Esperanza did not respond. They got out of the cab at the house of El Indio (who was also called the Black Bastard) and went into the alley where he lived. Esperanza and Bill wanted drugs. El Indio wasn't in. Bill took

off with Esperanza and the naive Jack stayed behind in the courtyard and waited for them. The little complex was "full of screaming
children and drunks and women with wash and banana peels." He
sat on a concrete step and started sketching the kids. Suddenly a
man appeared and offered Jack a glass of pulque, which Jack accepted—". . . it's one of my drinking days . . ." Then the man invited
him into a room, where a pitcher brimming with pulque stood on a
table. A fat woman, "like out of Rabelais and Rembrandt Middle
Ages," was singing accompanied by a guitarist. As in any group
there was a leader, this one looking like Pancho Villa: he had a "red
clay face, perfectly round and jocund, but Mexican owlish, with
crazy eyes . . . But beside him other more sinister lieutenants of some
sort . . ." Malevolently drooling, they were eager to mess with this
guileless outsider. The careless Jack chose that moment to ponder
the meaning of existence and tossed the grifters one of the key questions of universal philosophy: What is life? One of the group, practically pissing himself with laughter, invited the impetuous and now
drunk Jack Kerouac to the bathroom. While they were urinating,
the man pulled Jack's wallet from his pocket. Giggling, the disin-
genuous Jack asked him to give it back, which he did, but not before
removing some bills. Jack didn't do a damn thing about it! He didn't
joke, didn't get mad, didn't thrash the bastard or shoot a bullet into
his balls as William S. Burroughs would have. The Christian–Buddhist Jack was at the mercy of these hyenas, who were busy brewing
cultural-historical vengeance against the white intruder, a member
of the so unconsciously despised First World. As he went back into

the room, another urchin, sensing Jack's cluelessness, pulled a notebook from his coat containing recently written poems. Jack smiled childishly and asked him to give it back. But the grifter made off with it, perhaps sensing the stature of the writer in front of him. Jack never got his poems back. He masochistically confessed to himself: "... this is just a case of wanting to be robbed, a strange kind of exultation and drunken power." Whoa. Then, without further ado, he sang along with the group of misfits on those pain-wracked ballads that Mexicans are so fond of spewing—they're called *rancheras*— as feigned evidence of his great appreciation for their musical taste. But Jack lost his nerve and as he drank his pulque began to worry about his wallet and himself. Bad move, Jack. Until he got back from another trip to the bathroom and saw a "pale, slow, majestic" woman on the stairs. Esperanza. He thought she had come back to rescue him when in fact she was looking for drugs at El Indio's place. El Indio still hadn't arrived. When Esperanza decided to go, Jack followed her, continuing his odyssey through Mexico City's subterranean districts.

Very late, Jack and Esperanza left the complex and headed for Santa María la Redonda, a "slippery garbage street of dull brown cokestand lights and distant dim blue and rose neons." They met up with Cruz. "The three of us start off, and from the Golden Eternal Heaven bends God blessing us," related Jack the believer. They sat down at a snack stall and drank hot punch. As he'd been robbed, Jack didn't have any money. Esperanza paid. Suddenly she kissed his lips softly. At the end of the closed street, a policeman detained a vagrant. Dawn broke. The three were sleepy and the sisters needed to shoot up some morphine. They went into a seedy hotel full of whores and junkies. Esperanza and Cruz jabbed their forearms. Jack wanted to sleep with Esperanza there. "What interesting types!" said Jack, referring to the crowd that took opium and crashed at the hotel. Jack was certainly fond of the lower depths; he most likely came to Mexico to punish himself and pay a certain debt to his God. They left the hotel and walked toward a clandestine bar where they ordered drinks. Esperanza staged a parody of Jack shivering from the cold the whole evening and halfway through her performance she began to tremble, convulse, and writhe around on the floor. Some kind of attack. Jack and Cruz thought she was dying. Blood ran from her nose. At last she got over it and Jack and Cruz dragged her out of the place. They took a taxi to Garver's but he wouldn't let them in. They weren't wanted by the women of the complex. Jack hoped Esperanza would come in so he could take care of her and spend the night with her. But realizing they were being barred from the premises, the sisters caught a bus and split. Jack watched them receding into the distance and exclaimed:

> My poems stolen, my money stolen, my Tristessa dying, Mexicans buses trying to run me down, grit in the sky, agh, I never dreamed it could be this bad— (*Tristessa*, 84)

The next day Jack and Garver were talking things over when a trembling, bony hand appeared through a hole in the street-side wall. It was the bothersome hand of Esperanza, clamoring for drugs.

She begged Garver to open the door but he would not let her in. If he had, the women of the complex would have been quite alarmed; they were spooked by Esperanza. Jack and Garver went out to the street and saw the scabs on Esperanza's face. After the attack she'd suffered in the bar, she fell down another three times. The trio then headed for a bar, Esperanza, "wrapt in a purple shawl, skinny— poor,—like a vendor of loteria tickets in the street, like doom in Mexico." Without thinking, Jack told Esperanza that he loved her. Garver was stunned, Esperanza indifferent. They left the bar and went to Garver's place, somehow escaping the notice of the ladies in residence. Back up in the room, as they drank mezcal, Jack found out that Esperanza was more attached to Garver than to him. For the drugs. It was morphine rather than anything else that inexorably bonded them. Garver explained: "You put Grace Kelly in this chair, Muckymuck's morphine on that chair, Jack, I take the morphine." Esperanza topped that off: ". . . and me I no awanta love." Jack finally got the message, after the caresses, uncertainties, and anxieties, that he and Esperanza were on very different wavelengths.

But, despite the account he gave in *Tristessa*, Jack did make love to Esperanza, perhaps that same day, when instead of shooting up she stayed over to sleep in his rooftop room. There, sick and semiconscious, she lay on the mattress beside him as he practically forced her to have sex. This then was Jack's final farewell to Esperanza Villanueva—the most conspicuous Mexican character ever tied to a Beat writer—who then faded into the leaden depths of an ever-more sinister Mexico City.

In mid-October 1956, William S. Burroughs, then living in Tangier, Morocco, wrote Allen Ginsberg a letter with an invitation to visit. "DON'T GO TO MEXICO . . . COME RIGHT HERE RIGHT NOW WHILE YOU HAVE THE LOOT. TANGIER IS THE PLACE. WHY WAIT???" Ginsberg didn't go to North Africa but to Mexico City, to look for Jack. Accompanied by his lover, Peter Orlovsky, Peter's brother Lafcadio, and the shrewd, complicated poet Gregory Corso, he arrived at 210 Orizaba at the end of October. They rented an apartment next to Garver's and below the rooftop abode of Jack, who'd been awaiting them eagerly. A day after their arrival, Ginsberg went upstairs very early to wake Jack so they could go to the campus of the National University. Once aroused from his slumber Jack told him, wisely:

> "What do I care about Mexico City University, let me go sleep!"
> . . . "This is insane!" I yell. "I'll go with you to show you the Pyramids of Teotihuacan or something interesting, but dont drag me to this silly excursion." (*Desolation Angels*, 265–66)

Fine, Jack. Not the least bit interested in Mexico's higher education, not at all persuaded to explore the empty halls of Mexican intellectualism, Jack Kerouac, like Burroughs, was never interested in Mexican culture. Zero interest in the bookish writers of the time, zero interest in the painters, none whatsoever in the academics. He'd never even heard of Alfonso Reyes, Salvador Novo, Octavio Paz, or Juan Rulfo. The first would have reeked of urine from the library bathroom, the second of nail polish, the third of a tuxedo with mothballs in the pockets; he might've been interested in the fourth. He never admired the Mexican muralists, not even the hyper-propagandist frog Diego Rivera, whose soul could not be glimpsed without checking under the folds of his ample belly. He never signed up to yawn through a class at the National University or even at Mexico City College. He never read the newspapers, nor did he find out much about what was then going on at the national level. He did like, or pretended to like, Pérez Prado and the cha-cha-cha. Rather than well-regarded intellectuals, Jack sought out the rougher characters, the ones who lived on the edge.

Jack didn't want to go to the recently inaugurated Ciudad Universitaria, the campus of the National University. Why bother? They didn't teach poetry in the classrooms. But in the end, he did accompany his friends to the campus, and while the sociable Ginsberg combed the place for poets, Jack went to the library and read an article by Cocteau in French. Afterward they returned to the Roma district and, respectably attired, went to eat at the Kuku, at the corner of Avenida Insurgentes and Calle Coahuila, where Elias Breeskin (father to the cabaret star Olga Breeskin) played the violin. The restaurant (which closed its doors in 1996) had an excellent soup for just five pesos, enough to feed one for the whole day, and huge T-bone steaks with all the trimmings for eighty American cents. These they ate by candlelight and downed mugs of draft beer.

That night, fifteen-year-old Lafcadio Orlovsky was stricken with fever, convulsions, and nausea. Garver showed up, suggested giving him a shot of morphine as a cure, and they injected the boy in the arm. The next morning Lafcadio, like new, ran out to buy himself an ice cream. Garver was a good doctor.

Another day they took in the ruins of Teotihuacán, this time in tourist style. Beforehand they went to the Alameda and took the famous photo (the only one of Jack taken in Mexico) in which they're standing in front of a fountain looking gawky and drab—not at all like the prophets of an explosive generation. Arriving at the site where men are supposedly transformed into gods, they climbed the Pyramid of the Sun. "When we got to the top of the Pyramid I lit up a marijuana cigarette so we could all examine our instincts about the place." Then Jack accidentally cut his hand on a shard of broken glass left behind by a careless tourist. Later they entered the underground galleries where they clowned around as ghosts, smoked grass nonstop, and spent hours observing giant ants building their nests on the dusty ground. After concluding their entomological research, they returned contentedly to Mexico City. Their tour to the most highly energized pyramids in the Americas turned out to be not so mystical.

A few days later, Ginsberg, Peter, Corso, and Jack escaped to Plaza Garibaldi by night and went into the Bombay nightclub, domain of hookers and dancers for hire. Corso, after getting a whiff of Garibaldi's seedy, malodorous environs, chose not to go in, hailed a taxi, and went back alone. The other three entered the Bombay. Although the average Mexican male would have found the dance hall merry and fun—anything but shady—to Jack it was a disappointment:

In the Club Bombay are a dozen crazy Mexican girls dancing at a peso a throw with their pelvics tossed right into the men, sometimes holding the men by the pants, as an unbelievably melancholy orchestra trumpets out blue songs from the bandstand of sorrows—The trumpeters have no expression, the mambo drummer is bored, the singer thinks he's in Nogales serenading the stars but's only buried in the slums' slummiest hole agitating mud from our lips. (*Desolation Angels*, 273)

Almost immediately they left the ill-fated club and walked to the corner where some "mudlipped whores just around the slimy corner of the Bombay are standing ranked against pockholed walls full of bedbugs and cockroaches calling out to parades of lechers who prowl up and down trying to see what the girls look like in the dark." Jack and Peter picked out theirs and Ginsberg, arms crossed, waited outside. Jack had chosen a fourteen-year-old girl and Peter an obese, antediluvian number. The girl charged Kerouac three pesos (twenty-four cents). They entered the lair through a thin, worn-out curtain. The walls exuded dampness and a mattress was spread out on some boards within niches littered with religious icons and prayer cards. The Mexican girl turned out to be "so small you cant find her for at least a minute of probing." After Jack finished, he went out to the street and noticed "the awful smell of old fried sausages, brick smell, damp brick, mud, banana peels—and over a broken wall you see the stars." Here then is another faithful reflection of Jack's feelings about Mexico: amid all the filth, a light could be glimpsed. Meanwhile, Peter emerged from his encounter with the fat one, who, besides pleasure, gave him a case of gonorrhea, which he had cured a week later with injections of dihydrostreptomycin (penicillin G). The more fastidious Jack remained uninfected, as he'd cleaned up his organ with a special cream after having sex.

They left the hooker zone and, via Santa María la Redonda, arrived in the area for "beat (poor) Mexican nightlife." There they encountered an odd pair of street kids wearing makeup on their faces, all set for a performance (nothing new under the sun many years later in twenty-first-century Mexico) and met a gang of youths, who, aside from stealing and smoking marijuana, wrote poetry and discussed philosophy (including Husserl's phenomenology, my dear Jack?). Then and there Jack experienced a fit of nostalgia for his homeland and "It all makes you want to go back to America to Harry Truman's face." So much sordidness sickened him.

A day later, back at the flat, everyone was flabbergasted to see Gregory Corso packing his things. Gloomy, two-faced Mexico (whose culture he described as a blend of tacos and Pepsi) didn't much appeal to him; he found it boring. He complained of the dearth of luxuries, services, or even of any instances of madcap behavior worthy of the Beat leaders. "Why cant we even go ring the Cathedral bells at Midnight!" he asked. The next day, as Jack tells it, Peter, Ginsberg, and Corso went to the Zócalo, asked the guard at the Mexico City Cathedral for permission to climb up to the belfry, and there seized the bell ropes and clanged away. Mexico failed to heed their call.

The next day, Corso made roast beef in the oven, and in the

evening some rowdy medical students, amply supplied with mezcal (which Jack thought was unrefined tequila), joined them. They spent the whole night imbibing and even went to a brothel, though they weren't allowed in. But Corso couldn't take much more of Mexico and flew to Washington the very next day. Even so, several poems that he wrote in Mexico appeared in one of his best volumes, *Gasoline*. The poet took the disgust that Mexico induced in him and alchemically turned it into Beat free verse.

To wind up the tour, Gregory, Peter, and Jack went to Xochimilco, where they ate mole, got drunk on maguey sap—which Jack thought was unrefined mezcal—and then cutely got into a gondola. Oh, what a beautiful lake.

The phase of Jack's journey spent with his friends seems a rather trifling interlude. Jack fared better traveling solo than playing tour guide in Mexico. The mystical amazement that the land inspired in him never surfaced when he was with his chums, and his scenarios came out more journalistic, as when they gawked at the fireworks that night on the Zócalo (Jack said it was November 16, though it must have been the twentieth, anniversary of the disgraceful Mexican Revolution):

When the Mexicans have fireworks everybody stands there yelling OOO! . . . It's like war. Nobody cares. I saw a flaming wheel pirouetting down right on the crowd across the square. Men rushed away pushing baby carriages to safety. The Mexicans kept lighting madder and bigger stationary affairs that roared and hissed and exploded all over. (*Desolation Angels*, 281)

Back in the humid, gloomy atmosphere of 210 Orizaba, Allen Ginsberg and Jack Kerouac had a memorable conversation. Ginsberg suggested that Jack leave Mexico and return to New York. "It's time for you to make it! . . . Get published, meet everybody, make money, become a big international author, sign autographs for the old ladies in Ozone Park," Ginsberg told a skeptical Jack, who thought his work owed little to anyone. "All that literary stuff is just a drag," he responded to Ginsberg, who countered with an attempt to hit a nerve:

Where's your old Dostoyevsky curiosity? You've become so whiney! You're coming on like an old sick junkey sitting in a room in nowhere. It's time for you to wear berets and suddenly amaze everybody who's forgotten you're a big international author even celebrity. (*Desolation Angels*, 282)

Prophet Ginsberg finished off his harangue by inscribing one of the guiding themes of his literary life in gilded letters: "It's time for the poets to influence American Civilization!" Wow. Kerouac didn't much like the sound of this declaration of principles by the author of *Howl*. He found it ambitious, political, messianic (Jewish blood coursed through the veins of Jeremiah Ginsberg), and ultimately unrelated to the fundamental questions of mankind. "If you'd really seen a vision of eternity you wouldn't care about influencing American Civilization," he responded to Ginsberg, who continued to hold forth, arms flailing; he was quite fond of imaginary podiums. "'On the Road' is a big mad book that will change America! . . . Big

Faulkners and Hemingways will grow thoughtful thinking of you. It's time!" Jack didn't have the slightest intention of becoming a Beat messiah, a newly coined neo-prophet in a plaid shirt with rolled-up sleeves and a mop of unruly hair. It terrified him to play the captain of any ship that waved his flag, even one that symbolized his ideals. More individualistic than Allen, Jack had isolationist tendencies that would intensify over time. Jack Kerouac would never become a mobilizer of public opinion, as would Ginsberg, nor lead any street demonstrations, nor stage any spectacular acts against the war. His destiny was not to change the world but to hasten his departure from time, to flee from it, along the way bestowing an ungrateful humanity with some of the twentieth century's most abrasive literature.

Minus the angst or transcendental visions, Jack was able to get a different take on Mexico with his comrades in tow. He came down from his religious aeries to discover a cooler, more realistic profile of the Mexicans. As he developed this sensibility, the Jack Kerouac–Mexico bond turned less transcendental but more relaxed, less demanding but more congenial:

In my mind's eye I always remember Mexico as gay, exciting (especially at 4 P.M. when the summer thundershowers make people hurry over glistening sidewalks which reflect blue and rose neons, the hurrying Indian feet, the buses, raincoats, little dank groceries and shoe repairs, the sweet glee of the voices of the women and children, the stern excitement of the men who still look like Aztecs) ... But suddenly you see a fat Indian old lady in a shawl holding a little girl by the hand, they're going into the pastelería for bright pastries! The little girl is glad—It's only in Mexico, in the sweetness and innocence, birth and death seem at all worthwhile. (*Desolation Angels*, 248)

The final day of his stay in Mexico, in mid-December 1956, Jack, Allen, and sycophants planned to cut out like the maid, under cover of night, without saying good-bye to Bill Garver who was ill and could not go out. They preferred to avoid him, knowing he'd ask them to get morphine, which they had neither the time nor the inclination to accomplish. As they tiptoed out of the complex, Jack's good side got the better of him and he could not resist bidding Garver farewell for the last time. Hearing the unmistakable sound of his friend's voice, Garver begged him to go out and buy drugs. "I want you to go downtown do somethin for me—It wont take long. . . . you shouldnt leave me alone. Not like this especially not when I'm sick and cant raise my hand to find my cigarettes—. . . If you leave me like this this morning I'm goinna *die!*"

Old Garver's entreaties were useless and annoying to his not-exactly-faithful cohorts, who left him alone to whine and swear while they ran off like kids to the corner. There an Italian from New York, who taught language classes in Mexico City and looked like a Las Vegas gambler, awaited them in his car, ready to take them back to their country. Ginsberg had haggled over the price to cover the three thousand miles to New York. They never saw Garver again.

6

But I never dreamed, and even in spite of my great
determination, my experience in the arts of solitude, and my
poverty's freedom—I never dreamed I'd be taken in too
by the world's action—I didn't think it possible that—
—JACK KEROUAC, *Desolation Angels*

Back in New York, five minutes from fame, Jack got the news that Viking had accepted *On the Road* for publication—five years after he wrote it. There is never a shortage of astigmatic editors in this world. The mercenary Phoenicians of letters promised him an advance of a thousand dollars, which he gave Memère a few months later. Aware of emerging musical trends, Jack considered titling his novel *Rock 'n' Roll Road* but decided against it. In New York, he met Helen Elliot, a refined woman with whom he had a not-so-fleeting love affair that failed to develop, Jack typically reluctant to get involved. He was now downing torrents of Jack Daniels. Days before he left for Orlando to spend Christmas with his mother and sister, Ginsberg took him to the Russian Tea Room, where the clownish Catalan Salvador Dalí was taking tea with his wife Gala. Seeing Kerouac's face, Dalí told him he was more beautiful than Marlon Brando—who happened to be sitting at one of the nearby tables. Jack's hale and hearty appearance was not to last much longer.

After staying with his family for several weeks, during which he typed the drafts he'd written down in pencil in Mexico, Jack returned to New York, asked Ginsberg for a two-hundred-dollar loan, and, in February 1957, boarded a Yugoslav cargo ship bound for Tangier, Morocco, where he was going to visit Burroughs. Reading Kierkegaard's *Fear and Trembling*, weathering violent, boat-rocking storms, and sharing a cabin with a fat, homely woman supposedly spying for the secret service of the USSR, he finally arrived in Tangier. Burroughs was concentrating on *Naked Lunch*, and Jack helped him type it up. The two smoked hashish and hung out with European hipsters who Jack could not stand, and Jack visited prostitutes. They both awaited Allen Ginsberg and Peter Orlovsky, who arrived in March with the news that U.S. Customs had confiscated five hundred copies of *Howl*. With its simplicity and wide openness, fellahin Morocco appealed to Jack. People never stared at you ("unlike Mexico which is *all* eyes"). Even so, he departed earlier than expected and went to France, where he contemplated the land of his ancestors for the first time, reverently visited the Louvre, ate marvelous pastries, sobbed listening to a children's choir at the church, spent a few days with Gregory Corso, whom he overheard making love to a French girl at night, sat in cafés and people-watched. All that time he sought out not a single artist or intellectual. But he finally tired of France and took a ferry across the English Channel to London, where his local agent advanced him a few pounds for the publication of *On the Road* in England. Later he boarded the New York–bound *New Amsterdam,* an elegant steamer in which the preening, tuxedo-clad waiters scornfully eyed his urban cowboy outfit of jeans and frayed flannel shirt.

RAPTURE IN MEXICO

From New York, he hurried down to Orlando to get his mother, to whom he proposed they go to live in California, among other reasons because the sleuthing lawyers of Joan Haverty, still his legal wife, were trying to track him down. Memère accepted and they took the bus. Along the way they made a stop in New Orleans, and after drinking and enjoying themselves in several bars—at sixty-two, Memère could still booze it up—continued on their way west. Reaching El Paso, Jack could not resist crossing the border, going to Ciudad Juárez and showing it to his mother:

> Immediately we were in Mexico, that is, among Indians in an Indian earth—among the smells of mud, chickens, including that Chihuahua dust, lime peels, horses, straw, Indian weariness— The strong smell of cantinas, beer, dank—The smell of the market—and the sight of beautiful old Spanish churches rising in the sun with all their woeful majestical Maria Guadalupes and Crosses and cracks in the wall— (*Desolation Angels,* 383)

Driven by revelatory gusts and buffeted by profound spiritual agitation, Memère felt a wave of faith welling up in her belly and made up her mind to enter a church and light a candle for Jack's father. They crossed the threshold of the Juárez church, and breathed in the dense, smoky atmosphere. Suddenly, their retinas registered some ragged figures draped in discolored shawls crawling like devout caterpillars, with imploring arms raised toward the blue-indigo ceiling, and barefoot women toting children wrapped in smelly, tattered rebozos advancing on their knees toward the altar. "He's a *penitente*," Jack told his mom as he softly squeezed her arm, and proceeded to tell her the legend of the illiterate Juan, the one responsible for inventing Mexico's main myth, that of our ineffable, widely worshipped little virgin (sniff), María de Guadalupe. Jackie Kerouac, a *guadalupano* no less! (Which may take some effort to forgive.) The mournful fervor was contagious, and mother and child reverently approached the altar:

> We creeped up to the altar and lighted candles and put dimes in the church box to pay for the wax. Ma made a prayer to God and did the sign of the cross. The Chihuahua desert blew dust into the church. The little mother was still advancing on her knees with the infant quietly asleep in her arms. Memère's eyes blurred with tears. Now she understood Mexico and why I had come there so often even tho I'd get sick of dysentery or lose weight or get pale. (*Desolation Angels*, 384)

Standing beside his mother, one of his staunchest psychological pillars, Jack felt the religious sentiment that Mexico so inspired in him swirling around his imaginative head, given as he was to embroidering fantasies. What better way to retro-feed the Mexican magic than to witness Memère before him, so moved to observe the plain, unvarnished religious behavior of an underdeveloped country where poverty made Catholic ritual a gallery of collectible woes, pure eschatology, and visual atrocity. Such was the impact of Memère's visit to the church in Juárez that years later, tells Jack, she prayed daily for the fate of that long-suffering Mexican mother who crawled to the altar on her knees.

Of course, Mexico also had its quaint, playful side. In Ciudad Juárez's horrendous central square they saw a man with a soothsaying bird. Memère paid a peso and wanted to know her fortune. The bird grabbed a little piece of folded paper with its beak and gave it to the proprietor: "You will have goods fortuna with one who is your son who love you," it read, to the amazement of the foreign lady. She thought the son in question was Gerard, who had died at age eight, rather than Jack, who this time took no offense. He was soaking it all up, watching his mother make her discoveries like a girl flustered by something new in a country so close to the USA yet so different. That afternoon they got a bottle of bourbon and polished it off in the bus to California.

In Berkeley Jack sometimes saw Neal, who was now deeply into horse racing. A hysterical Carolyn told Jack that his presence did harm to her innocent husband and that she was against their seeing each other. He also went to visit Philip Whalen and other poets from the Beat pack. But Memère didn't like California and, like Jack, felt restless and wanted to go somewhere else. They packed their things and decided to go back to Florida with Nin. Just a day before their departure, the postman knocked on the door. Jack opened it to receive a boxful of copies of *On the Road*. Whoa. After a five-year wait, Jack's stomach contorted like a clam sprinkled with sulfuric acid.

Once in the bookstores, *On the Road* left its creator's hands and fell prey to both the media, with its voracious tarantulas and rapacious piranhas, and the hordes of young people who saw in him a marvelous source of ethical identity. Both responses surpassed Jack's expectations, and he wasn't prepared to deal with either the betrayals or the bitter fruit of celebrity.

WHEN THE EARTH SHOOK

On the soul-corroding threshold of fame, Jack spent a few days in Florida with Memère and his sister, then, as if warming up for a harsh future, in late July lone traveler Jack caught a Greyhound bus from Florida to Matamoros and dropped down into "Gloom Mexico," as he now called it. Arriving at 210 Orizaba, he received the sad if not unexpected news that Bill Garver had died a month earlier. But there was more: Esperanza was no longer living where she used to and could not be found anywhere. Life had swallowed her up. Lacking his usual contacts, Jack went to the Luis Moya Hotel in the center of town, which he called the Marble Hotel in *Desolation Angels:* "an old 1910 whorehouse built of solid marble & tile & not one crack in our walls." A search down Calle de Panamá brought new disappointment: the whores had been cleared away, apparently owing to the influx of Americans in the zone. Back at the Luis Moya,

Jack started writing an article titled "On the Beat Generation," in which, inspired by certain ideas from *The Decline of the West*, he pointed out that Spengler had foretold the rise of a new religious spirit of the sort incarnated by the Beat Generation. Meanwhile, he awaited the arrival in Mexico of a new lover, the novelist Joyce Glassman, but she never showed up. To top it off, on Sunday, July 28, 1957, at 2:40 in the morning while he was sleeping, Jack felt the ground beneath him moving—for a change, not existentially:

> . . . the hotel room is rocking like a ship—It's a giant earthquake rocking Mexico . . . It's all over. I . . . jump under the bed to protect myself against falling ceilings if any . . . The entire apartment building across the street from the post office on Calle Obregon is falling in killing everybody—Graves leer under Moon pines—It's all over. (*Desolation Angels*, 409)

Apart from toppling the Angel of Independence monument, the quake of '57 also demolished a building located at the south corner of Álvaro Obregón and Frontera, opposite the post office, a mere three months after it was constructed. (Incidentally, the author of the book that you hold in your hands is at this moment looking through the window at that very same fateful corner, now occupied by a mediocre, by-the-hour hotel.) As the Luis Moya Hotel was quite a distance from there, Jack could not have witnessed the building's collapse. When describing his experiences, he didn't always stick to the truth; rather, he liked to juggle the facts, play around with events, and, riffing like a jazz soloist, let it all flow through the pages. His truth was not a matter of respecting the "objectivity" of his experience but of achieving a deep, cinematic literary intensity.

"It's all over," Jack rightly put it after the earthquake that took seventy lives. His trip to Mexico was a string of catastrophes that culminated with the quake. He stuck around Mexico City for a few more days—two weeks in all—where it was "one horror after another as usual." Then, scared, alone, sick with the flu, his testicles swollen, he packed his things and, before catching a bus to Florida, wrote the poem "Mexican Loneliness." A bad trip.

> And I am an unhappy stranger
> grooking in the streets of Mexico—
> My friends have died on me, my
> lovers disappeared, my whores banned,
> my bed rocked and heaved by
> earthquake—and no holy weed
>> to get high by candlelight
>> and dream—only fumes of buses,
> dust storms, and maids peeking at me
>> thru a hole in the door
>> secretly drilled to watch
>> masturbators fuck pillows—
>
>> . . .

7

Physical laws are millstones; if you cannot
be the miller you must be the grain.

—ÉLIPHAS LÉVI, *Transcendental Magic*

After Jack returned from Mexico in August 1957, his life suddenly came off the hinges. Jack had foreseen it—as one traveling down a river hears the rumbling of the next set of cascades—but he'd never imagined that fame would hit him so hard or that it would be so difficult to navigate the straits of celebrity. Jack wasn't ready to confront the situation that the span of his work would inevitably entail: his conversion into a writer-prophet who symbolized irreverence, rebellion, and the consequences of it. Jack was as lucid as he was weak. His unbalanced state resulted from the difficulty of living up to his conscience. His survival instincts could not keep up with the speed and prowess of his discoveries, visions, and prophecies. His nervous system lagged behind his vertiginous, lucid spirit. Spiritual dyslexia. His soul ran faster than his body, and life cost him dearly. "His giant wings kept him from moving," as Baudelaire put it. And to protect himself, Jack continued boozing, taking drugs, radiating antisociability, and taking refuge under Memère's petticoats.

With the appearance of *On the Road* in 1957, followed by *The Subterraneans* and *Book of Dreams*, and with the widely propagated myth of the Beats (*beatniks*, as the *San Francisco Chronicle* dubbed them, after the fashion of using -*nik*, of the Soviet Sputnik, actually a diminutive and derogatory suffix from Yiddish), a hail of criticism assailed Jack Kerouac's life. The American media and critics were put off by his work and attitudes. They'd never drunk from this well before. Not knowing what to make of his writing, they simply put it down and distorted it. Most critics were unable to forgive him for eschewing what they deemed literature. Jack was anything but a writer, they said, or no more than a typist, as pipsqueak Truman Capote judged him. His style was flat, literal, boring, they went on, the themes of his writing dangerously unconventional, a call for ir-reverence. True, there was the odd academic or journalist who praised his work but they were few and far between. Jack was prey to the media, who treated him like a crazed misfit, a piece of mer-chandise to be sold. In interviews, one after another imbecilic TV broadcaster (is there any other kind?) attempted to minimize his work and image. Sadly, Jack often showed up at the studio drunk and played the fool. North American society could not forgive him for questioning its conformist-puritanical-pragmatic tribal codes and did everything possible to neutralize and caricature him and put him in a shop window with a sign reading, "Look at the silly man, he wants to be different from us." And the childlike Jack lacked the guile to elude all the mean-spiritedness, didn't have the strength to avoid their sharpened fangs, as did Allen Ginsberg, William Burroughs, or Bob Dylan. The hypersensitive, skittish Jack had neither the courage nor the demeanor to keep from being destroyed by them, and instead of arming himself to face whatever new challenges life might throw his way, he succumbed, let himself fall to the ground. He never really attempted to kick his detractors in the ass, whether by the tip of his shoe or by studied indifference, and there he lay on indignant ground and never rose, wishing for a speedy demise. He couldn't even take refuge in Catholicism, which in the end proved ineffective for him, nor in Buddhism, which no longer excited him. God, Christ, and Buddha were all useless to him. Instead, he took consolation in the only course he deemed viable: suicide by obsessive alcoholism—a prolonged but certain prescription.

Nor was Jack buoyed by the enormous acceptance of his book and legend by thousands of young men and women across the world. On the contrary, he refused to become the heraldic angel for a set of values and attitudes that challenged the asphyxiating, insubstantial behavioral codes of the developed West. Despite his misgivings, he was being elevated by young people to the role of ringmaster of a new age, as if he had access to marvelous, uncharted territory. In making his mark, Kerouac sacrificed himself as a person—as forced to by caustic, dictatorial spirits. He paid his karmic debt with interest and in the process gave as much away as he did himself harm. Here was another paradox of Jack Kerouac: he was a prophet in spite of himself who remained woefully unaware of his own actions. Realizing what his work and legend had unleashed, he preferred to keep a low profile and decline the role of gifted writer and maker of splendid dreams.

And while Jack was being thrashed by the hurricanes of fame, his alter ego, Neal Cassady, was following a similar course. Neal, who also drank and used drugs indiscriminately and had turned his marriage to Carolyn into a living hell, was thrown in jail for dealing marijuana. From then on his life took a precipitously self-destructive turn (Jack never visited him in jail nor helped out with the bail payments). However much he was the incarnation of life-affirming jazz, the supreme improviser of experiential phrasing, Cassady could no longer take the hairpin turns of existence either. Even the jazz life has its rules, though neither Neal nor Jack ever considered them. In the end, life conquered them both and, sick of it all, they gave it the finger and raised their glasses to the only remaining retreat: death. It was the infallible absolute they both deep down yearned for. Better to vanish from an undesirable world that could not contain their energies, where their lust for life had proved insatiable and their passions never took root. At the end of the road death awaited, the sooner the better. The destination wasn't too hard to find.

Jack kept writing (he never stopped), though not in the same vein as during his heroic years; and he kept drinking, like a wayward man of the steppes, becoming the butt of countless bar brawls (once a gay man beat him senseless outside a New York bar, claiming he had been portrayed in *The Subterraneans* without permission). Jack continued to isolate himself with help from Memère. Fearing her son would become ensnared in the subversive adventures of Ginsberg and his henchmen, she sent the poet a letter threatening to report him to the FBI if he came near her defenseless son. (Unlike Kerouac,

Ginsberg embraced the role of Beat leader, protesting, agitating, and broadcasting his ideas to the four winds while he mocked the media and used it as he pleased.) Surprisingly enough, Jack basically concurred with his mother's view, though he did not refrain from seeing Allen. Scared stiff of being imprisoned for petty crimes as Neal had been, or for the subversive content of his books, Jack almost completely suspended his usual travels, and in his final years practically never left the house or Memère's lap. He went so far as to say he would never travel again as he did with Neal on those "stupid roads."

For the first time in his life Jack was making enough money to buy his adored/loathed mother a house near New York. (Lucien Carr told of how during a dinner he attended, the ambivalent Jack called her a "dirty whore.") A sense of financial well-being may have depleted his capacity for creativity. Meanwhile, he continued to have fleeting relationships with women like Joyce Glassman and Dodie Müller without getting too involved, and continued to be hounded by the mother of his daughter, who never stopped asking for money.

Along this grim stretch of the road, Jack made his last detour to Mexico.

AT THE END OF THE ROAD

In late June 1961, Jack Kerouac, who had moved with Memère to Orlando, Florida, got a flight to Mexico City. Gone were the romanticism and adventurous discomfort that a journey to the magical south had always entailed. Jack rented the old apartment at 37 Cerrada de Medellín, where Burroughs had lived in 1950, thus closing a cycle of Mexico residences by staying in the same place he'd occupied when he first arrived there.

He got right to work on a second part to *Desolation Angels*, compiling a volume of fifty thousand words. One day he went into the corner shop and the clerk, a loutish character, told him straight to his face that he loved him. Jack suggested the man buy him a drink and they apparently had an affair though there's little evidence of it. Guillermo, the shop clerk, invited Jack to the cinema so they could enjoy seeing some of the leading men of the era: Pedro Armendáriz, Pedro Infante, Arturo de Córdova, etc., but to Jack their barrel-shaped torsos held scant appeal. Jack's suitor further plied him with seconals and grass and held forth about Santa Teresa de Jesús and San Juan de la Cruz.

The assertion that Jack came to Mexico, among other reasons, to punish himself rings true. Guillermo invited some of his buddies to Jack's place, and they proceeded to steal his razor, his Buddhist beads, his flashlight, and his suitcase. When they grabbed his raincoat, Jack begged them not to take it, saying his mother would scold him if she found out about it. The lowlifes found this hilarious; they didn't give a damn and took everything. Jack never learned his lesson about how Mexicans dealt with foreigners. Deep down, he surely despised and disdained Mexicans, but his odd, perennial desire to idealize clouded even his survival instincts. No matter how much he was lashed by cold reality, Jack Kerouac remained attached to his chimeras, fantasies, and subliminal ideas about a country that only existed in his obstinately imaginative head.

Shortly before leaving, he chose to lock himself away and plunge into the only waters where he could swim well, without undue risk: writing. This time it was series of poems in the form of choruses, which he titled "Cerrada Medellín Blues." In the sixth chorus the outlines of his mood came right through:

> Alone with my Guardian Angel
> Alone in Innisfree
> Alone in Mexico
> City
> Alone with Benedict,
> Cave is free,
> alone is alone,
> Thou Only One—
> Alone and Alone
> The song of the pree
> (Pree means prayer
> in English & Frenchie)
> Choose yr words lightly,
> shit on the world,
> Merton'll die
> when he reads
> this from me

Afterward, Jack got a flight back to Florida to be with Memère. Over the next eight years left to him on the planet, he never once returned to "the hot country" of "the desert rats and the tequila." The transcendental fantasies he'd conjured up about Mexico were of no more use to him. He no longer took refuge in a country so different from his own. The magic and innocence of Mexico were forgotten, and all that remained was a distant cloud of dust at the end of the road.

THE FINAL HITCH

The rest of the story is outside the scope of this book. Suffice to say that in the last years of his life, Jack Kerouac sealed his own fate, succumbing to an inexorable suicidal inertia that he never quite shook off. Isolated from his road buddies, shut away with his mother and in the last three years with his wife Stella Sampas, sister to his teenage friend Sammy, reluctant to get involved in the ethical movement that his books engendered, among other things, drinking relentlessly, picking fights in bars, playing the fool in the media, writing without his old fire or jazzistic precision, Jack allowed time to disenchant his soul and wear down his body. On October 21, 1969, he left his house in St. Petersburg without saying good-bye to his wife, walked to the highway, and stood on the shoulder. No sooner had he lifted his thumb than a black car stopped and a cold, bony hand signaled him to get in. Jack ran over to the car and got in. The driver headed straight for a land of which Jack never wrote a word. It was his last trip. He was forty-seven.

The wise doctors, who treat men like bundles of viscera, secretions, and bones, diagnosed him with hemorrhage of the esophagus. Jack Kerouac's deplorable physical condition was the cause of his death, the clods concluded. How simple it is to reduce the end of earthly life to a physiological dysfunction! Fools! Especially in the case of a poet abducted by heteroclitic, ungovernable visionary forces that were as physical as a hungry wolf is tender. But modern medicine has no concern for the spirit; it's all a matter of bodily and glandular clockwork. In their view, men, even poetic geniuses like Jack Kerouac, are nothing but mechanized skin.

A year and a half before Jack died, the jazz solo incarnate, if now a tired and cacophonous one, reached his definitive end. In February 1968, Neal Cassady—who Kerouac disdained and saw little of in his final years—was found dead by the railroad tracks in San Miguel de Allende, Mexico, after having taken an unfortunate mixture of alcohol, pills, and marijuana. He was forty-two.

Jack never recognized his daughter Janet, whom he saw only twice, though he finally agreed to help her mother with a few dollars a month. The grown-up "Jan" followed in her father's slippery steps—much as Burroughs's son had. From very early on, she consumed enormous quantities of drugs, took several risky journeys to Mexico, even whored herself, and wrote several novels in autobiographical style. She died in 1996 at age forty-four.

Memère, that leathery pelican, confined to a wheelchair, paralyzed but triumphant, outlived her three children (Jack's older sister Nin died in 1964) and passed away in 1971.

In April 1997, Allen Ginsberg, by that time a legendary figure, died of liver cancer in New York at age seventy-one, and later that same year, William S. Burroughs, the last surviving member of the trinity, died of a heart attack at age eighty-three, in Lawrence, Kansas.

No doubt the souls of Kerouac, Ginsberg, and Burroughs are enjoying their stay on freer, subtler planes of existence (where they can get away with anything but the imprudence of writing) than this unsavory physical one, which, rest assured, dear reader, is just a stop along the way.

THE DISGUISE OF INNOCENCE

Not all works of literature possess *spirit*. Some are merely the sum of well-arranged words, others ideas dressed up as fiction. The works of Dostoyevsky, Melville, Pessoa, and Jack Kerouac were all rooted in *spirit*. Works created by spiritual writers breathe subtly from deep within. Because of this, their creations are essentially superior to those by other writers who, rather than plumbing the depths of themselves to create their work, strive for stylistic perfection or doctrinaire sermonizing. The works of Faulkner, Capote, and Dos Passos lack spirit: they aim chiefly to deliver ideas in a pretty package, not to express something from their souls. Only lightweights posing as aesthetes or those inclined to believe anything would suggest otherwise.

Jack was not fond of the world in which he lived and did anything possible to get away from it. His sensibility and genius ran against human convention. The world is the realm of the finite, of failure, of pain, but also of Jack Kerouac himself and the conflictive, tortuous stuff he was made of. In hating the world, Jack hated that part of himself that remained shackled to suffering, uncertainty, or guilt. Gifted with literary genius, Kerouac wanted to exorcise his inner demons by writing and strove desperately to transcend the existential planes of his being without ever managing to. Over time, Jack became aware of the uselessness of writing. But apart from the fact that he didn't know what else he could do, it provided him a measure of solace, among other reasons because he knew the value and transcendence of his work.

The paradox of Jack Kerouac the writer is that, instead of fleeing from his experiences, he attempted to re-create them, trace them, as if in giving them form on paper his life would be cleansed, purified, transformed into something absolute. In this case, literature was true revenge against the inconvenience of existence. Unlike Beckett or Burroughs, Jack Kerouac the writer wasn't escaping from himself by creating his own universe but attempting to rescue life through literature, to claim ownership of it in the only realm where he remained ruler of himself and demiurge: writing.

Spirit in the work of Kerouac is most apparent where he attempted to reconcile the smallness of human beings with their yearning for spiritual transcendence, hell with heaven. Few authors, not even mystics, have achieved this. In Kerouac's books, depravation and the search for God are one and the same. He never excluded one from the other. A drunken binge was a part, not the negation, of spiritual ascension. Of course, Jack Kerouac was incapable of living in accordance with this spirit.

The author of *On the Road* saw his life transformed after surviving a sort of shipwreck that left him stranded in Mexico. Kerouac turned to "the magic land" to the south essentially to escape the suffocation of his own country. Ever prone to fantasy, he tended to idealize a nation with an ad hoc culture as an answer to the hyper-materialistic civilization of the USA. Particularly during his early trips, Mexico was a holy, redemptive zone, a mystical ground where the innocence of people before God appeared in even the pestilent corners of Plaza Garibaldi. Kerouac was desperate to find a spiritual climate that could release him from himself. This he easily achieved, inclined as he was to imagine a Mexico that only existed in his neurons. In short, Jack *made* a Mexico to the measure of his inner chimeras and boiled it down to a fiction that helped him survive at the time.

Which is not to say Jack didn't notice the meanness of Mexico. Most of his literary chronicles do in fact emphasize the sordidness and violence of its cactus-sphere. But such was his multidimensional fellahin Mexico, so willing was he to forgive its squalor, so great was his need for a cultural, religious antidote to his own country that he never dared so much as to wink at its ugliness. I have no doubt that at times Kerouac deeply despised the Mexican milieu. But never, I insist, did he ever curl his fingers inward, raise his powerful fist to deliver a physical or verbal blow to any malicious Mexican jaw. Damn it, Jack, wouldn't it have been great to do just that?

To Kerouac, traveling to Mexico was less of a risk than living in his own country. In Mexico he was safe from all the machinery that revolved around him as a writer: the fame, the nobodies, the voraciousness of the media, the critics, the generational commitments, the money, the self-esteem: in the USA, he had no choice but to face the whole set of challenges and confrontations that would assail him. Kerouac went to Mexico to taste the hot sauce, which although it might burn he knew wouldn't kill him. Going to Mexico was a dangerous game but not a lethal one. The risk Jack ran living on Mexican soil was not so innocent as it appeared. He approached it with a wary eye, knowing where and when to get involved with people and the precise moment to get away. Realizing that the risks were not so serious, he sometimes played the victim as a way to absolve himself of the guilt that besieged him, but his game was suspiciously fictitious. Jack's supposed innocence in Mexico was a disguise that concealed a double dissimulation: he avoided *real* challenges in his own country while pretending to confront them in the fellahin land to the south. For Kerouac, Mexico wasn't so much a magical place as a form of therapeutic calisthenics, if not consciously so.

Not only did Jack feign his own innocence, but he also cast Mexico in that same role, working up a whole fable in which Mexicans were spiritual, sacrosanct, pure, quasi-divine. Off this innocent stage, his disguise could never work. Perhaps because of this he never railed against Mexico. Doing so would have made his own "innocence" seem false. So this was a double case of feigned innocence: that of Kerouac himself and the one that he imposed on Mexico.

In the last eight years of his life, Kerouac forgot about Mexico. Buried beneath a thanatological avalanche, he hoped only for death, and in this trancelike state Mexico ceased to be the lifesaver it once had been—a precarious and chimerical but ultimately useful one. After he renounced life and allowed himself to be devoured by the implacable jaws of his own country, Mexico no longer made any sense. There was no point in continuing to grant it such superlative qualities, no reason to dress it up in marvelous disguises. When Jack surrendered his will to live according to his ideals, Mexico vanished off the map of his fantasies. At that moment, the fireworks he'd imagined in his dream state ceased to shine so brightly . . . and never again could he cry out, even in profound sadness: ¡Viva México!

Quotations of Jack Kerouac's writing were taken from the following books. In chapter 2, *On the Road* (New York: Viking Press, 2007) and *Visions of Cody* (New York: Penguin Books, 1993). In chapter 3, *Lonesome Traveler* (New York: Panther/Granada Publishing, 1979). In chapters 3, 5, and 6, *Desolation Angels* (New York: G. P. Putnam's Sons, 1978), In chapter 4, *Tristessa* (New York: McGraw-Hill, 1978). In chapter 6, *Book of Blues* (New York: Penguin, 1995). Quotations from Kerouac's letters are from *Jack Kerouac: Selected Letters, Volume 1, 1940–1956,* edited by Ann Charters (New York: Viking, 1995) and *Volume 2, 1957–1969* (New York: Viking, 1999). Other books by Kerouac referred to in the text are *Dr. Sax* (New York: Grove Press, 1994); *Book of Dreams* (San Francisco: City Lights Books, 1981); *The Dharma Bums* (New York: Penguin Books, 1986); and *Vanity of Duluoz* (London: Quartet Books, 1977).

Several biographies of Kerouac were consulted: Gerald Nicosia, *Memory Babe* (New York: Grove Press, 1984); Ann Charters, *Kerouac: A Biography* (New York: St. Martin's Press, 1987); Dennis McNally, *Desolate Angel: Jack Kerouac, the Beat Generation, and America* (New York: McGraw-Hill, 1989); and Barry Gifford and Lawrence Lee, *Jack's Book: An Oral Biography of Jack Kerouac* (New York: St. Martin's Press, 1994).

Quotations of William S. Burroughs were taken from *The Letters of William S. Burroughs, 1945–1959,* edited by Oliver Harris (New York: Viking, 1993); *Tornado Valley* (New York: Cherry Valley Editions, 1989); and William S. Burroughs, *The Adding Machine: Selected Essays* (New York: Grove Press, 1986).

Other books consulted include Walter Allen, *The Urgent West: The American Dream and Modern Man* (New York: Dutton, 1969); Ralph Waldo Emerson, *Essays of Ralph Waldo Emerson* (London: Franklin Watts, 1969); Walt Whitman, *Leaves of Grass* (New York: Modern Library, 1950); Carolyn Cassady, *Off the Road* (New York: William Morrow and Company, 1990); C.W. Leadbetter, *Buddhism* (Whitefish, Mont.: Kessinger Publishing LLC, 2010); Oswald Spengler, *The Decline of the West* (New York: Alfred A. Knopf, 1946); Edgar Tavares López, *Colonia Roma* (Mexico City: Editorial Clío, 1998); Éliphas Lévi, *Transcendental Magic: Its Doctrine and Ritual* (Cambridge: Cambridge University Press, 2013); Aleister Crowley, *The Confessions of Aleister Crowley* (London: Penguin [Non-Classics], 1989]); and Vladimir Mayakovsky, *Mi descubrimiento de América, Obras completas,* vol. 2 (Buenos Aires: Editorial Platina, 1959). The Mexican newspapers *El Universal* and *Excelsior,* especially from 1950, 1955, and 1957, were also consulted.

JORGE GARCÍA-ROBLES
is a Mexican novelist, critic, and translator; he is considered the
leading authority on the Beats in Mexico. He is the author of
The Stray Bullet: William S. Burroughs in Mexico (Minnesota,
2013). He translated Jack Kerouac's *Lonesome Traveler, Tristessa,
Mexico City Blues, Maggie Cassidy,* and "Cerrada Medellín Blues"
and William S. Burroughs's *The Yage Letters* into Spanish.

DANIEL C. SCHECHTER
is an American writer and translator living in the Netherlands.
He is the translator of *The Stray Bullet: William S. Burroughs
in Mexico* (Minnesota, 2013) and has translated for the
Mexican publications *Artes de México* and *Escala,* as well
as contributing to many Lonely Planet guidebooks.